THE MAGIC LENS

Volume 1

HOME SCHOOL EDITION

by

Michael Clay Thompson

Royal Fireworks Press

Unionville, New York

Royal Fireworks Press
First Avenue, PO Box 399
Unionville, NY 10988-0399
TEL: (845) 726-4444
FAX: (845) 726-3824
email: rfpress@frontiernet.net

ISBN: 0-88092-581-7

Printed in the United States of America on acid-free, recycled paper
using soy-based inks by the Royal Fireworks Printing Company
of Unionville, New York.

Table of Contents

The Magic Lens

A Guide for Parents

The Magic Lens grammar program is designed to break the barriers of traditional instruction in grammar. Rather than repeating the Big Myth, that grammar is a boring, remedial, unteachable subject, *The Magic Lens* confirms what we have known deep down all along: grammar is an exciting form of higher order thinking about language, and a subject that is perfectly teachable. Grammar is a way of thinking about our own ideas.

As a bonus, *The Magic Lens* is now coordinated with *The Word Within the Word* vocabulary program. For anyone who does not use *The Word Within the Word*, there is no harm; *The Magic Lens* stands alone beautifully, but for those who do use *The Word Within the Word*, they will find their vocabulary from that program featured in *The Magic Lens*, where the same words can be seen as phenomena of grammar, thus reinforcing both programs, the words and their usage.

One goal of *The Magic Lens* is to rebuild the grammar calendar. Instead of dragging out grammar instruction until the end of the year—a well intentioned plan but one that prevents students from ever applying grammar, since you can't use what you don't teach until May—*The Magic Lens* provides a compacted approach, presenting all four levels of traditional grammar (parts of speech, parts of sentence, phrases, and clauses) in the first weeks of school. It is not a grammar unit; it is a grammar *launch*. Once the grammar is put in place, *The Magic Lens* provides a wide array of grammar experiences that enhance students' understanding for the rest of the year, and that lets them apply their four levels of grammar to all other language arts experiences.

How is it possible to compact a so-called year's worth of grammar into a month? First, we discover that the supposed immensity and difficulty of grammar are exaggerated. There are really only fifty or sixty terms that students need in order to master the fundamentals of traditional grammar. It is a tiny microsubject of great power. Second, if you put yourself through ten pages of exercises every time you learn a new term, then anything will take years. In *The Magic Lens*, we don't stop learning every time we encounter a new word. Instead, we learn in sets and batches of terms that go together, and instead of dozens of isolated exercises that confine themselves exclusively to a single term, we use four-level analysis. In four-level analysis, we study not one term, such as *preposition*, but an entire sentence. We examine a sentence, and we determine the part of speech of every word, all the parts of the sentence, the phrases, and the clauses. We take a complete look. So every time we find a new sentence to examine, the process is a *thumbnail review of all of grammar*! Look closely at the chart and diagram on the following page:

	Every	planet	has	a	magnetic	field	around	it.
Parts of Speech:	adj.	n.	v.	adj.	adj.	n.	prep.	pron.
Parts of Sentence:		subject	predicate			direct object		
Phrases:							--prepositional--	
Clauses:	one independent clause, simple declarative sentence							

Prepositional phrases are always modifiers: adjectives or adverbs. How do we know that this phrase is an adverb and not an adjective? We can hear the logic: it has it around it, sounds more right than a field around it. And the phrase tells where the planet *has* it.

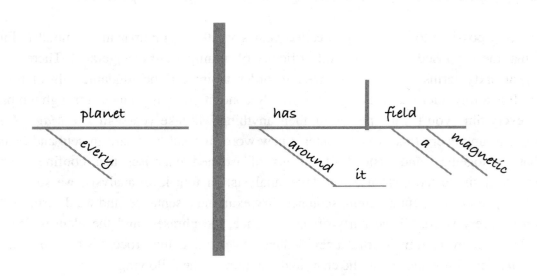

Just imagine what you will accomplish if your student can work through that chart and diagram before the end of September. And then imagine how rapidly the clarity will increase after you have done ten, and twenty, and thirty such sentences! In the traditional program, it takes until May to get to clauses, and students only really have one chance to learn each thing as it is studied and then rapidly abandoned. In *The Magic Lens*, students learn all the concepts up front quickly, and then review them over, and over, and over, every time they do a four-level analysis of a sentence.

The Magic Lens is divided into two real sections, first the introductory lectures, and then the loops. All of the main concepts are provided in the introductory lectures; once you have completed that section, the loops continue to build comprehension by looping repeatedly back through the concepts, providing different ways of thinking about them, as well as incredible sentences that can only be fully appreciated with the *Magic Lens* of grammar.

Some recommendations for using *The Magic Lens*:

• Adopt a consistently positive and enthusiastic approach. Never say bad things about grammar, such as that it "might not be fun but you have to do it." Grammar IS fun, and exciting, and very, very learnable.

• Emphasize always how easy grammar is. After all, there are only eight parts of speech, and two sides of a sentence, and several kinds of phrases, and really two kinds of clauses. How hard can it possibly be? Grammar has been made to seem much harder than it really is.

• Be Socratic. In other words, as the teacher, you should often confine yourself to questions, and let the student work through the thought processes. Avoid saying *yes* or *no* very much. If a student says that a word in a sentence is an adverb, when you know it is an adjective, don't say *no*, just ask, "Well, what does it modify?" In this way, the student will realize that it can't be an adverb, and will figure it out on his or her own. You want the solution to come up within the student's own mind, rather than in your own. Student realizations must be internal, and not transfer from us in an authoritarian way. By using questions, in a respectful and supportive tone, you can guide the process so that the maximum benefit occurs. We can also be Socratic by selecting sentences that are so challenging that the correct interpretation is in doubt, period. Those make some of the best and most exciting sentences, when several interpretations are competing for our decision.

• Use a grammar catechism. You saw the four-level grammar chart above. Make your own by picking a sentence, writing it on board or paper, and drawing four lines beneath it. Then go through the sentence with questions, letting the student provide answers. Here is an example of the kind of thing that I have always done in the classroom:

The Catechism

The process goes something like this: I write a sentence on the board. Let us say that the sentence I write on the board is:

The Andromedans attacked savagely, and we fell back.

The Andromedans attacked savagely, and we fell back.

Teacher: Here we go. This is one of the sentences on your grammar test, so let's go through it together. We will do a four-level analysis, and you take notes to study for the test. Feel free to ask questions. Today, just call out your answers to my questions. Ready?

Students: Yes.

Teacher: What's grammar?

Students: A way of thinking about language.

Teacher: How many levels are there in traditional grammar?

Students: Four.

Teacher: What is the first level?

Students: Parts of speech.

Teacher: What are the parts of speech?

Students: The eight kinds of words in our language.

Teacher: Thanks. Let's do the parts of speech of all of the words in this sentence. What part of speech is *The*?

Students: An adjective.

Teacher: What kind of adjective?

Students: A definite article.

Teacher: What does *The* modify?

Students: *Andromedans*.

Teacher: What part of speech is *Andromedans*?

Students: A noun.

Teacher: What kind?

Students: A proper, plural noun.

Teacher: What part of speech is *attacked*?

Students: A verb.

Teacher: Action or linking?

Students: Action.

Teacher: Transitive or intransitive or neither?

Students: Intransitive.

Teacher: Why is it intransitive?

Students: It's an action verb without a direct object.

Teacher: What tense is it?

Students: Past tense.

Teacher: Is it active voice or passive voice?

Students: Active voice.

Teacher: How do you know *attacked* is active voice?

Student: Because the verb is voiced so that the subject is acting.

Teacher: Good. What part of speech is *savagely*?

Students: An adverb.

Teacher: What does it modify?

Students: *Attacked.*

Teacher: Prove to me that *savagely* doesn't modify *Andromedans.*

Students: Adverbs don't modify nouns.

Teacher: What modifies nouns?

Students: Adjectives.

Teacher: What part of speech is *and*?

Students: A conjunction.

Teacher: What kind of conjunction?

Students: Coordinating.

Teacher: List the coordinating conjunctions.

Students: And, but, or, nor, for, so, yet.

Teacher: What two things does *and* coordinate in this sentence?

Students: Two independent clauses.

Teacher: Good. We'll look at that more closely in a minute. What part of speech is *we*?

Students: A pronoun

Teacher: An object or subject pronoun?

Students: A subject pronoun.

Teacher: Why is it a subject pronoun?

Students: It's the subject of a predicate.

Teacher: What person and number is *we*?

Students: First person, plural.

Teacher: What is *we*'s antecedent?

Students: *Andromedans.*

Teacher: We are the Andromedans?

Students: No.

Teacher: Then what does *we* replace?

Students: You can't tell from this sentence.

Teacher: Right. The antecedent is unknown. What part of speech is *fell*?

Students: A verb.

Teacher: Is *fell* action or linking?

Students: Action.

Teacher: Transitive or intransitive?

Students: Intransitive.

Teacher: What tense is *fell*?

Students: Past tense.

Teacher: Active voice or passive voice?

Students: Active.

Teacher: Good. What part of speech is *back*?

Students: A preposition.

Teacher: What is the object of that preposition?

Students: Oh. It's not a preposition, it's an adverb.

Teacher: If it's an adverb, what does it modify?

Students: .

Teacher: Prove to me that it's not an adjective.

Students: Adjectives don't modify verbs.

Teacher: What do adjectives modify?

Students: Nouns and pronouns.

Teacher: Good. That finishes the parts of speech. Are there any questions about the parts of speech in this sentence before we look at the second level of grammar? . . . OK, what is the second level of grammar?

Students: Parts of the sentence.

Teacher: What is a sentence?

Students: A thought.

Teacher: No.

Students: Yes.

Teacher: Prove it.

Student: In a sentence, you say something about something, and that is what a thought is.

Teacher: OK, then what are the two important parts of each thought?

Students: The complete subject and the complete predicate.

Teacher: What part of this sentence shall we look for first?

Students: A subject.

Teacher: Do you see a subject?

Students: *Andromedans.*

Teacher: What is that subject's predicate?

Students: *Attacked.*

Teacher: Once again, is it action or linking?

Students: Action.

Teacher: Therefore, what are we not looking for?

Students: A subject complement.

Teacher: Why are we not looking for a subject complement?

Students: Subject complements go with linking verbs.

Teacher: Then what are we looking for?

Students: A direct object.

Teacher: Is there a direct object?

Students: No.

Teacher: Isn't *savagely* a direct object?

Students: No, direct objects are nouns or object pronouns.

Teacher: Is there an indirect object?

Students: No.

Teacher: How do you know?

Students: There's no direct object.

Teacher: So what?

Students: The indirect object comes between an action verb and a direct object.

Teacher: Is there another subject or are we through?

Students: *We* is a another subject.

Teacher: What predicate is *We* the subject of?

Students: *Fell.*

Teacher: Is *fell* action or linking?

Students: Action.

Teacher: So what are we not looking for?

Students: A subject complement.

Teacher: What are we looking for?

Students: A direct object.

Teacher: Is there one?

Students: No.

Teacher: How do you know?

Students: Nothing receives the action.

Teacher: Are we through with parts of the sentence?

Students: Yes.

Teacher: Do you have any questions, before we go on to the third level of grammar? . . . What is the third level of grammar?

Students: Phrases.

Teacher: What is a phrase?

Students: A group of words that doesn't have a subject and its predicate, and that is used as a single part of speech.

Teacher: What kinds of phrases will we look for?

Students: Prepositional, appositive, and verbal.

Teacher: Any prepositional phrases in this sentence?

Students: No.

Teacher: Any appositive phrases?

Students: No.

Teacher: What's an appositive phrase?

Students: An interrupting definition.

Teacher: Isn't *we fell back* an appositive phrase?

Students: No, its an independent clause.

Teacher: Are there any verbal phrases?

Students: No.

Teacher: Isn't *attacked* a participle?

Students: No, it's a verb, not an adjective.

Teacher: No gerunds?

Students: No, there are no *-ing* words.

Teacher: Are there any questions about phrases before we go to the fourth level of grammar? I would be happy to go over anything you'd like.

Student: Can a participle end in *-ing*?

Teacher: Good question. Yes, a participle can end in many things, including *-ing*. If I say, "Falling suddenly, Starbuck yelped," the word *Falling* is a participle modifying the noun *Starbuck*. Does that make sense?

Student: Yes.

Teacher: Good. Thanks for your question. Any other questions? . . . What is the fourth level of grammar?

Students: Clauses.

Teacher: What is a clause?

Students: A group of words with a subject and a predicate.

Teacher: What clauses do you see in this sentence?

Students: Two independent clauses.

Teacher: What's the first clause?

Students: *The Andromedans attacked savagely.*

Teacher: What's the second?

Students: *We fell back.*

Teacher: What is the sentence structure?

Students: Compound.

Teacher: How do you know it isn't complex?

Students: There is no dependent clause.

Teacher: What is the punctuation rule for this kind of compound sentence?

Students: I,ccI. (Pronounced, "eye-comma-see-see-eye.")

Teacher: Explain the I,ccI rule.

Student: Put a comma before a coordinating conjunction in a compound sentence.

Teacher: Good, thanks. What is the sentence purpose?

Students: Declarative.

Teacher: Thanks. That was a good analysis. Before we go to the next test sentence, are there any questions?

Students: . . .

Teacher: . . .

Students: . . .

Teacher: Ok, let's look at the next sentence on the test. (Writes the next sentence on the board.) Here we go again! What is grammar?

Students: A way of thinking about language.

Teacher: What are the four levels of traditional grammar?

Students: Parts of speech, parts of the sentence, phrases, and clauses.

Teacher: What are the parts of speech?

Students: The eight kinds of words.

Teacher: What part of speech is this first word . . . .

The first sentence took five minutes or so, and now it begins again, sentence by sentence, using each sentence as a model and review of grammar. As a teacher, you ask essentially the same questions every time: all of the parts of speech, all of the parts of the sentence, all of the phrases, and all of the clauses. Challenge the students to prove their points; make them explain their decisions; make them identify their nouns, their pronouns, their conjunctions; ask them what is joined by the conjunction, what is modified by the modifier, what is replaced by the pronoun. Ask them why the sentence is punctuated as it is. When they make a mistake, you accept the answer with a straight face, and ask them a following question that allows them to figure out for themselves that they made a mistake. *They* have to solve the problems. And when you have completely analyzed the sentence, you begin all over again: "What is grammar?"

If you are using *The Magic Lens* but not *The Word Within the Word*, you will enjoy seeing the advanced vocabulary that is used to make grammar examples. The student will benefit tremendously just from the exposure to these words. If you like, you can create some activities in which the student looks up some of those words and explains what the sentences mean. On the other hand, if you are also using *The Word Within the Word*, then you will see that Lists 1-10 of *The Word Within the Word* coordinate with the introductory lectures in *Magic Lens*, Lists 11-20 go with Loops 1-5, and Lists 21-30 go with Loops 6-10. It's simple. And since the *Word Within the Word*-based quizzes already appear in the student book of *The Magic Lens*, you don't even have to run anything off or try to figure out where it goes. It's all done.

What is not in the student book is the set of review tests that follow Loops 1-5 and 6-10; those are included below for you, together with answer keys.

I hope you and your student thoroughly enjoy using *The Magic Lens*. It has taken decades of classroom experience and years of writing to make this available in this form, and I know that a knowledge of grammar is one of the most exciting and beneficial things that can be studied. Have fun learning.

In the sentences below, the words in **bold** contain important Latin or Greek stems. Which of the words in bold are nouns? For each **bold** word that is a noun, write *noun* in the blank to the right.

1. The Civil War **antedates** the Korean War by decades. _____

2. The **anti-aircraft** fire shot down the enemy planes. _____

3. The two nations have a **bilateral** agreement. _____

4. The **circumspect** spy is difficult to catch. _____

5. The two together are an interesting **combination.**   noun

6. Stubb was **confined** to the ship's hold. _____

7. The lunar lander **descended** through the atmosphere. _____

8. Queequeg's attention was not easily **distracted**. _____

9. She made an **equilateral** triangle with three straws. _____

10. It was an **extraordinary** achievement. _____

11. They were lost in **interstellar** space. _____

12. He received an **intravenous** solution through a tube in his arm. _____

13. The boy was a lonely **introvert** who kept to himself.   noun

14. He looked fearfully at the glowing, **malevolent** demon. _____

15. Ishmael had the **misfortune** to forget his wallet.   noun

16. The Pequod's voyage is not a **nonprofit** endeavor. _____

17. Flask added a **postscript** at the bottom of the letter.   noun

18. Before Romeo left, Juliet had a frightening **premonition**.   noun

19. The circle was divided into two equal **semicircles**.   noun

20. The Ahab a sharp order to her **subordinate**.   noun

In the sentences below, the words in **bold** contain important Latin or Greek stems. Many of the sentences also contain pronouns, though they are not in **bold**. Underline each pronoun you see, and in the blank at the right, write in the type of pronoun it is: subject, object, demonstrative, etc.

1. It is, or once was, ruled by a **monarchy.**   subject

2. The **dullard** was always boring everyone to tears.   indefinite

3. In killing his father, Oedipus was guilty of **patricide.**   possessive

4. She is an electronic **technician.**   subject

5. The **dermatitis** on his skin was painful and unpleasant.   possessive

6. Balthazar, the scuba diver, collects them—**aquatic** species.   object

7. The deaf moose had injured his **auditory** nerve.   possessive

8. **Belligerent** nations gain nothing from their many wars.   possessive

9. The hostile island tribe **captured** them.   object

10. He **incised** the design into the oaken door with a knife.   subject

11. **Biomorphic** abstract sculpture resembles these.   demonstrative

12. Patton wrote a tedious **autobiography** about his exploits.   possessive

13. The **porter** will carry your bags to the train.   possessive

14. Please **inscribe** my yearbook.   possessive

15. Since Ishmael loved insects, he studied **entomology.**   subject

16. The grand jury returned a robbery **indictment** against him.   object

17. A **credulous** person will believe that.   demonstrative

18. Fortunately, the **centipede** wears its shoes.   possessive

19. Ishmael was a **neophyte** in whaling, but he learned quickly.   subject

20. He, Ahab, was a lifelong **bibliophile.**   subject

In the sentences below, the words in **bold** contain important Latin or Greek stems. The words in *italics*, including those in both bold and italics, are the subject of this exercise. For each word in italics, write either *noun* or *adjective* in the blank at the right.

1. English contains *many* **homophones** like two and too.   adjective

2. It was a ***specious*** argument, but it sounded convincing.   adjective

3. The *callow* youth was **inducted** into the army.   adjective

4. The **transfer** was made in the darkness of a *moonless* night.   adjective

5. The patent is still **pending** on the secret *product*.   noun

6. The *two* bacteria were only a **micron** apart.   adjective

7. The fire **hydrant** stood in *front* of the school.   noun

8. An overexposure to *the* sun's **photons** gave her a sunburn.   adjective

9. The swift god Apollo was a member of the *Greek* **pantheon**.   adjective

10. He wore a **pentagram** on his sleeve, not an *ordinary* pentagon.   adjective

11. The strange boy could move distant objects by ***telekinesis***.   noun

12. The wild creature had an ***omnivorous*** appetite.   adjective

13. The surgeon was able to **excise** the *malignant* tissue.   adjective

14. Johann Sebastian Bach composed ***polyphonic*** music.   adjective

15. The crash victims suffered ***hypothermia*** on the frozen tundra.   noun

16. The amoeba uses its *flowing* **pseudopods** to move.   adjective

17. The human brain is said to contain over 100 *billion* **neurons**.   adjective

18. Iron ore is called ***hematite*** because of its red color.   noun

19. *Single-celled* animals are known as the **Protozoa**.   adjective

20. Laws against ***vivisection*** prevent cruelty to animals.   noun

In these sentences, the words in **bold** contain important Latin or Greek stems. Other words are in *italics*. For each word in *italics*, write either *noun*, *adjective*, or *verb* in the blank at the right. If it is a verb, also put *A* for action or *L* for linking.

1.   The crystal dissolved into an ***amorphous*** mass.   adjective

2.   The silk ***vestments*** were hanging on pegs.   noun

3.   Pip finally *knew* the name of his generous **benefactor**.   verb, A

4.   The **ponderous** burden *was* nearly impossible to lift.   verb, L

5.   His ***corpulent*** body was a result of his love of sweets.   adjective

6.   The evil creature *lay* **dormant** for centuries.   verb, A

7.   There *was* a birthday party for the venerable **patriarch**.   verb, L

8.   The recently *invented* laser toothbrush is a **novel** idea.   adjective

9.   Her ***punctilious*** attention to small details was impressive.   adjective

10.   Silver *felt* **dejected** when the expedition left without him.   verb, A

11.   The ***devastation*** intensified our need for creation.   noun

12.   *Self-motivated* people have an internal **locus** of control.   adjective

13.   The many-cultured United States *is* a **heterodox** nation.   verb, L

14.   The **amphibians** emerging from the water *had* impermeable skin.   verb, A

15.   Alexander's ***magnanimous*** victory speech was inspiring.   adjective

16.   The *euphony* of Mozart's concerto carried us away.   noun

17.   Human beings *have* **endoskeletons**, not exoskeletons.   verb, A

18.   The tremulous dog on the twenty-third floor has ***acrophobia***.   noun

19.   The **orthodontist** *straightened* Count Dracula's fangs.   verb, A

20.   The massive **megalith** *towered* over the ancient ruins.   verb, A

For each sentence, identify the part of speech of the word in *italics*.

1. In the spring of 2215, New York was a ***revitalized*** city.   adjective
2. The theory of ***democracy*** was proven very effective.   noun
3. If there is ***stereophonic*** sound, can there be stereo smell?   adjective
4. Is ***capitalism*** the opposite of Marxism?   noun
5. The poet was traveling ***incognito*** to avoid recognition.   adverb
6. The economic disasters could not be *readily* **surmounted**.   adverb
7. The senator's **sonorous** voice was *easily* her best weapon.   adverb
8. If the **asteroid** struck *the* earth, it would be a **disaster**.   adjective
9. Her **dynamic** personality made her an *obvious* choice.   adjective
10. Please **synchronize** your chronometers *immediately*.   adverb
11. The *very* hyperactive child suddenly began to **hyperventilate**.   adverb
12. The astronomer was an ***amiable*** individual.   adjective
13. The ***octarchy*** unanimously decided to invade Macedonia.   noun
14. The dancers' spinning **gyrations** *continued* long into the night.   verb
15. Their **contradictory** remarks *really* offered a sharp contrast.   adverb
16. Which do you *prefer*, geography or **geophysics**?   verb
17. Galileo thought that the solar system was ***heliocentric***.   adjective
18. The **thermotropic** plants were *suddenly* killed by the cold front.   adverb
19. Is a *square* a tetragon or just a **tetrahedron**?   noun
20. The **hydrometer** *accurately* measured the flow of the trout stream.   adverb

For each sentence below, identify the part of speech of the word in *italics*.

1.   His irrelevant comments were not **germane** *to* the discussion.   preposition

2.   The friendly alien proved to be *well-mannered* and **gregarious**.   adjective

3.   The mariner steered *through* beautiful **ultramarine** waters.   preposition

4.   The anthropologist loved ***primates***, most of the time.   noun

5.   The **pyromaniac** loved starting fires *with* pyrogenic materials.   preposition

6.   The loudmouth's ***clamorous*** cries could be heard for blocks.   adjective

7.   The candidate received a **plurality** but not a majority *of* votes.   preposition

8.   The job has many ***tangible*** benefits for a young person.   adjective

9.   The regulations were *too* **stringent** for the footloose, creative artist.   adverb

10. Did the Emancipation Proclamation ***liberate*** the slaves?   verb

11. There was a jungle *near* the **junction** of the Brazilian highways.   preposition

12. Would you rather be **excluded** *from* the new group?   preposition

13. There was a decision to **secede** *from* the Union.   preposition

14. The Amazon has many **tributaries** flowing *into* it.   preposition

15. Don't **dignify** his unworthy question *with* an answer.   preposition

16. Your **lucid** remarks clarified the confusing issue *for* everyone.   preposition

17. The ***eruption*** of Vesuvius disrupted our celebration.   noun

18. The man *beside* him was certainly no **ingrate**.   preposition

19. For Cicero, it was a **mediocre** speech, neither *excellent* nor poor.   adjective

20. The **translucent** material allowed us to see on the *other* side.   adjective

For each sentence below, identify the part of speech of the word in italics. If it is a conjunction, identify the type.

1. Please **enumerate** *and* explain your reasons.   conj., coordinating

2. Her character is one of great *personal* **fortitude**.   adjective

3. The **osteologist** was called *in* for consultation or referral.   adverb

4. **Ornithology** is a science is *for* the bird lovers of the world.   preposition

5. **Metropolitan** policy required the police to be polite *but* firm.   conj. coordinating

6. The stubborn old man *refused* to have the blood **transfusion**.   verb

7. He was *not only* egocentric, *but also* an **egomaniac**.   conj. correlative

8. The *ancient* poet was **inspired** by the Muse of poetry.   adjective

9. Ralph disputed the dialogue, *so* he received a **diatribe**.   conj. coordinating

10. The **acrimonious** dispute was *disturbing* to everyone.   adjective

11. The culprit was **exculpated** *and* escaped punishment.   conj. coordinating

12. A **pachyderm** *rarely* suffers from dermatitis on its trunk.   adverb

13. *When* it opens, will the zoo have a **protozoan** exhibit?   conj. subordinating

14. The perforations let water **percolate** *and* pass through the membrane. conj. coordinating

15. The **pacifists** were not pacified *by* the militaristic speech.   preposition

16. *Neither* **demagogues** *nor* pedagogues are to blame.   conj. correlative

17. *If* you have **necrophobia**, avoid the necropolis.   conj. subordinating

18. *Since* you ask, the wealthy **urbanite** had urbane manners.   conj. subordinating

19. *Because* he had a **pugnacious** attitude, he was repugnant to others.   conj. subordinating

20. **Ectothermic** species *and* others enjoy the summer warmth.   conj. coordinating

For each sentence, identify the part of speech of the word in italics.

1.	*Yes*, his **sedentary** job left him weak and out of shape.	interjection
2.	The ***illegible*** handwriting said, "Oh, I give up."	adjective
3.	*Wow*, the bitter animosity made him lose his **equanimity**.	interjection
4.	No, the ***tortuous*** highway was torture to drive.	adjective
5.	Yep, NATO, RADAR, *SCUBA*, and OPEC are **acronyms**.	noun
6.	Gee, the principles of democracy are ***sacrosanct***.	adjective
7.	Why, the werewolf is famous for his ***metamorphosis***.	noun
8.	*Wow*, the **Petrified** Forest is a desert?	interjection
9.	*After* the surgery, it was a **miracle** to look in the mirror.	conjunction
10.	After the ***manual*** labor, she needed a **manicure**.	adjective
11.	*Ugh*! Follow the **directions**, if you want correct answers.	interjection
12.	Golly, the noisy crowd made ***vociferous*** objections.	adjective
13.	*Dang*, the **demigod** drank from a dainty demitasse cup.	adjective
14.	Fooey, the class reunion left me in a ***retrospective*** mood.	adjective
15.	The explorer could **sense** the edge of the cliff. *Whew*!	interjection
16.	Yeah, it is time to **solidify** the gains *we* have made.	pronoun
17.	*Nope*, primates are known for **binocular** vision.	interjection
18.	Oh, the **curator** of the museum cared for the *Polynesian* artwork.	adjective
19.	*Jeepers*, you like **ultramarine** more than ultraviolet?	interjection
20.	*Well*, what does an **android** resemble?	interjection

17

In these sentences, each word in **bold** contains important Latin or Greek stems. First, identify the part of speech of the bold word, then identify the part of sentence of the word in italics, using the following abbreviations: subject, subj.; predicate, pred.; direct object, D.O., indirect object, I.O.; and subject complement, S.C. Your blank might look like: ___adv. D.O.___

1.	The **pathetic** creature received *sympathy*.	adjective, D.O
2.	The unexpected **anomaly** was *amorphous* in shape.	noun, S.C
3.	This is the *difference* between **astronomy** and agronomy?	noun, S.C.
4.	Does a **diffident** person have *self-confidence*?	adjective, D.O.
5.	Does **cacophony** hurt the *ear*?	noun, D.O.
6.	The **heterogeneous** mixture had a noisome *odor*.	adjective, D.O.
7.	Should *science* give us **prescience**?	noun, D.O.
8.	Would you like a *photograph* of my **autograph**?	noun, D.O.
9.	Is this treaty **bilateral** or *multilateral*?	adjective, S.C.
10.	The shiny red **tractor** attracted many *buyers*.	noun, D.O.
11.	Please **inscribe** *something* insane in my annual.	verb, D.O.
12.	*He* refused **to cooperate** with the copilot.	noun, subj.
13.	The **audiophile** has a wonderful *collection* of recordings.	noun, D.O.
14.	The **crystalline** *substance* began to evaporate.	adjective, subj.
15.	Did the **neolithic** *age* come before the paleolithic age?	adjective, subj.
16.	Can you find a *hexagram* and a **hexagon**?	noun, D.O.
17.	It's an *infraction* of the rules to fracture someone's nose.	noun, S.C.
18.	The **platypus** has a plate-like *bill*.	noun, D.O.
19.	The Greek **pantheon** of gods was not *monotheistic*.	noun, S.C.
20.	Can an ambulatory hospital *patient* **somnambulate**?	verb, subj.

For each of these sentences, first identify the part of speech of the word in **bold**, then identify the kind of phrase that is in italics.

1. The **orthopedist** went *on an expedition*. noun, prep.

2. Dr. Garcia, *the new mortician*, was **mortified** at the wound. adjective, appos.

3. The **carnivorous** beasts *of the plains* lived well. adjective, prep.

4. The **psychologist** viewed the parapsychologist *with suspicion*. noun, prep.

5. *Contradicting democratic philosophy,* **Ethnocentrism** injures all. noun, participial

6. The geneticist's hobby was *to study* **pathogenic** *substances*. adjective, infinitive

7. **Prenatal** care is important *to those in natural environments*. adjective, prep.

8. The **paleontologist** was an expert *on the Paleozoic era*. noun, prep.

9. To talk glibly gives only **cursory** attention *to the problem*. adjective, prep.

10. The **cryptologist** worked all night *to break the enemy code*. noun, infinitive

11. *Cracked lengthwise,* the object was discovered near the **cascade**. noun, participial

12. *Decapitating criminals* was once a common form of punishment. noun, gerund

13. The **loquacious** bore answered *with a circumlocution*. adjective, prep.

14. *From the beginning* the hero's sacrifice was a **sacrosanct** memory. adjective, prep.

15. The **United** Planets soon celebrate *forming their union*. adjective, gerund

16. The sky's **redness** streamed high *over the Himalayas*. noun, prep.

17. The **altimeter**, *rusted shut*, no longer measured the altitude. noun, participial

18. Computer **graphics** enhance books *on politics and economics*. noun, prep.

19. The **isothermal** foothills escaped the extremes *of temperature*. adjective, prep.

20. The new convert soon **reverted** *to his previous views*. verb, prep.

Use the grammar clues to solve this Mystery Sentence:

A children's story contains a compound declarative sentence distinguished by three independent clauses. A coordinating conjunction is used twice to join the three clauses together. Each clause contains a contraction of the first person singular subject pronoun and the helping verb *will*. The third clause contains a second person singular possessive adjective, a direct object, and an adverb. The first two clauses contain only subjects and verbs. What is the sentence?

---

1. I'll huff, and I'll puff, and I'll blow your house down.

For the next ten sentences, identify the **part of speech** of the word in **bold**:

1.	Do **bacilli** and fungi have nuclei in their cells?	noun
2.	Can a system of justice **ever** be unjust?	adverb
3.	The **luminous** moonlight illuminated the Pequod.	adjective
4.	The **superannuated** doorman celebrated his fiftieth anniversary.	adjective
5.	At the satellite's **apogee** we could not find it with binoculars.	noun
6.	The senior class president **befriended** the venerable man.	verb
7.	**On** his solo transcontinental flight, he enjoyed the solitude.	preposition
8.	Basic instructions are **included** with each new bassoon.	adjective
9.	The interrogation was **derogatory** in tone.	adjective
10.	Several members of **Parliament** had a parley in the parlor.	noun

For the next ten sentences, identify the **part of sentence** of the word in **bold**:

11.	The **plenipotentiary** met twice with the potentate.	subject
12.	The surge of the sea portended the **resurgence** of violence.	direct object
13.	The philologist delighted in inventing witty **neologisms**.	object of a gerund
14.	The grammar in the telegram was not **correct**.	subject complement
15.	During the holy man's incantation, the spirit began **to appear**.	direct object
16.	There **were** no regal ceremonies in the interregnum.	predicate
17.	The doctor's prognosis gave **Diogenes** renewed hope.	indirect object
18.	The musician's androgynous **appearance** was widely imitated.	subject
19.	The secret agent spilled the deadly chemical **agent**.	direct object
20.	There may be little **time** to act or react.	subject complement

For the next ten sentences, identify the **bold** phrase and its part of speech:

1.   Bulgakov, **the anarchist's friend**, had a severe case of anemia.   appositive, adjective

2.   **Complaining loudly**, the absentee landlord was abducted.   participial, adjective

3.   We advised the adventurer **to admire his adversary**.   infinitive, noun

4.   The melodeon played a sappy melody **during the melodrama**.   prepositional, adverb

5.   The pilot tried **to study aeronautics and aerodynamics**.   infinitive, noun

6.   The albino stared **at the white pages** of the blank album.   prepositional, adverb

7.   Luciferase is the enzyme **in the luminous organs** of the firefly.   prepositional, adjective

8.   Does Franklin's epitaph contain a witty epigram **for posterity**?   prepositional, adjective

9.   **At the exhumation**, the rich humus was removed.   prepositional, adverb

10.   **Viewing microbes** is a favorite habit of biologists.   gerund, noun

For the next ten sentences, identify the sentence structure (disregard bold type).

11.   The bonny lass discovered the **bonanza** by accident.   simple

12.   We learned, and the **superstructure** was constructed in three days.   compound

13.   They left when chlorine damaged the **chlorophyll** in the plants.   complex

14.   He held the **cyanotype** to the light, and she admired the blue lines.   compound

15.   The **cytologist** watched the leucocytes and erythrocytes.   simple

16.   She folded the **diploma** and handed it to the waiting diplomat.   simple

17.   His **dyslexia** made it hard to pronounce words, but he succeeded.   compound

18.   The **ecologist** was fascinated with living things in the ecosystem.   simple

19.   The senator had **hypoglycemia**, not anemia, when this occurred.   complex

20.   A specialist in dysentery and **enteritis** explained the rare ailment.   simple

For each of the following sentences, circle the letter of each answer that is true. The answer can be any combination, including all or none. This exercise will teach you the real process of punctuation as a function of grammar.

1. In October the Allies advanced and the Axis gathered its resources.

    a. a comma after the prepositional phrase

    b. a comma after the dependent clause

    c. a comma after the independent clause

    d. an apostrophe in the contraction

    e. commas before and after the appositive

2. In San Antonio Texas the tumbleweed covered Ricardos field.

    a. a comma after the city

    b. a comma after the state appositive

    c. an apostrophe in the plural noun

    d. an apostrophe in the possessive noun

    e. a comma after the dependent clause

3. A very large moon shone as Alexander the Macedonian conqueror rode forward.

    a. a comma between adjectives

    b. a comma after the dependent clause

    c. a comma after the independent clause

    d. commas around the appositive

    e. commas around the noun of direct address

4. Hamlet Whitmans book Leaves of Brass is about a train called The Occident Express.

    a. italics on the train title

    b. an apostrophe in the possessive noun

    c. quotation marks around the book title

    d. italics on the book title

    e. commas around the appositive

5. The well planned party and the serene weather rejuvenated twenty seven friends.

    a. comma between adjectives that precede the noun.

    b. a hyphen in the compound adjective

    c. a comma after the dependent clause

    d. a hyphen in the compound number

    e. an apostrophe in the possessive noun

Answer Key

1. In October the Allies advanced, and the Axis gathered its resources.
      a. a comma after the prepositional phrase   d. an apostrophe in the contraction
      b. a comma after the dependent clause   e. commas before and after the appositive
      c. a comma after the independent clause

   The sentence needs an I,ccI comma to make the sentence compound rather than run-on.

2. In San Antonio, Texas, the tumbleweed covered Ricardo's field.
      a. a comma after the city   **d. an apostrophe in the possessive noun**
      b. a comma after the state appositive   e. a comma after the dependent clause
      c. an apostrophe in the plural noun

   The state is an appositive, and needs a comma both before and after it, since it is an interrupting definition. We also need an apostrophe for the possessive noun.

3. A very large moon shone as Alexander, the Macedonian conqueror, rode forward.
      a. a comma between adjectives   **d. commas around the appositive**
      b. a comma after the dependent clause   e. commas around the noun of direct address
      c. a comma after the independent clause

   We need commas around the appositive, but not before the second clause, since this is an ID complex sentence. If it were reversed, then it would need the D,I comma.

4. Hamlet Whitman's book, *Leaves of Brass*, is about a train called *The Occident Express*.
      a. italics on the train title   **d. italics on the book title**
      b. an apostrophe in the possessive noun   **e. commas around the appositive**
      c. quotation marks around the book title

   Book titles and all major vessels of transport titles should be in italics (or underlined, same thing.)

5. The well-planned party and the serene weather rejuvenated twenty-seven friends.
      a. comma between adjectives that precede the noun.   **d. a hyphen in the compound number**
      b. a hyphen in the compound adjective   e. an apostrophe in the possessive noun
      c. a comma after the dependent clause

Use the grammar clues to solve this Mystery Sentence:

This sentence from a nursery rhyme begins with four alliterated one-syllable interjections in a row, followed by a first person singular subject pronoun, an present tense transitive action verb, a definite article, a singular common noun, a preposition that does not show a relationship of time or of space, an indefinite article, and a three-syllable proper noun.

Fee, fi, fo fum, I smell the blood of an Englishman.

For each of the next ten sentences, identify the **part of speech** of the word in **bold**:

1. **Polychrome** sculptures have more colors than monochrome ones.   adjective

2. The **formation** of troops in formal uniforms was impressive.   noun

3. Three consecutive sequels were of no **consequence**.   noun

4. **His** hypoglycemia made him watch his diet.   pronoun

5. The patient's hemophilia made it difficult to stop **the** hemorrhage.   adjective

6. The expedition's Ultima Thule was the **north** pole.   adjective

7. She felt that it was **infra dig** to eat fried chicken with her fingers.   noun

8. Leukemia produces an **excessive** number of leucocytes.   adjective

9. If **hemolysis** breaks down red blood cells, what does analysis do?   noun

10. Did mesons strike Mesopotamia in the **Mesozoic** Era?   adjective

For each of the next ten sentences, identify the **part of sentence** of the word in **bold**:

11. Would **you** walk a millimeter to drink a milligram of milk?   subject

12. The memo helped **him** remember the commemoration ceremony.   direct object

13. Don't digress; discuss **progress** with members of congress.   direct object

14. The collaborators spent laborious **nights** in the laboratory.   direct object

15. The myocardiograph showed his myocardium is **strong**.   subject complement

16. The evacuation left **vacancies** in the vacation resort.   direct object

17. The oligarchy gave national **policy** a renewed secrecy.   indirect object

18. Did the fructose from the apples raise his glucose **level**?   direct object

19. Unfortunately, the neurosis **developed** into a psychosis.   predicate

20. The celebrity's **pulchritude** was only equaled by his turpitude.   subject

For the next ten sentences, identify the **bold** phrase and its part of speech:

1. A pleochroic crystal shows colors **from different directions**. prepositional, adverb

2. **Quivering with anger**, the podiatrist treated the injured arthropod. participial, adjective

3. The sorority was located **between two fraternities**. prepositional, adverb

4. **Careful searching** showed not one phenomenon but several. gerund, noun

5. The valedictory address contained valid arguments **to think about**. infinitive, adjective

6. **Finally trapped**, the parapsychologist told a parable with a paradox. participial, adjective

7. Von Helmsmit, **the old baron**, was dominant over his dominion. appositive, adjective

8. Do workers **in this country** want a meritocracy or an ergatocracy? prepositional, adjective

9. Rhizophagous animals dig up and feed **on delicious rhizomes**. prepositional, adverb

10. Saprogenic bacteria caused the material **to decay rapidly**. infinitive, adverb

For the next ten sentences, identify the sentence structure (disregard the bold type):

11. The **schism** in the party healed, and they won the election. compound

12. When he's in **Mesopotamia**, he uses the **hippodrome**. complex

13. Did his **chromosome** problem have a **psychosomatic** cause? simple

14. The **Sporozoa** are **Protozoa**; they multiply by **sporogenesis**. compound

15. The people in the **station** voted to preserve the **status quo**. simple

16. As we climbed, **rhododendron** bloomed on the high mountainsides. complex

17. The **taxidermist** was interested in a new **taxonomy** of species. simple

18. The new **volunteer** had a **malevolent** expression if you ask me. complex

19. As the candidate tried to **fraternize**, the local politicians laughed. complex

20. **Trichinosis** is a disease; it is caused by the **trichina** worm. compound

For each of the following sentences, circle the letter of each answer that is true. The answer can be any combination, including all or none. This exercise will teach you the real process of punctuation as a function of grammar.

1. With a subtle sort of smile the president said All citizens are created equal.
   - a. a comma after the prepositional phrases
   - b. an apostrophe in the contraction
   - c. a comma before the direct quotation
   - d. quotation marks around the direct quotation
   - e. a period inside the closing quotation marks

2. When the poet wrote The Divine Comedy he created a new poetic form.
   - a. a comma after the independent clause
   - b. an apostrophe in the possessive noun
   - c. a comma after the dependent clause
   - d. italics on the poem title
   - e. quotation marks around the poem title

3. A two thirds Roman majority wanted circuses bread and gladiatorial entertainment.
   - a. a hyphen in the compound adjective
   - b. a colon at the beginning of the list
   - c. a comma after the plural common noun
   - d. a list comma before the coordinating conjunction
   - e. a comma after the dependent clause

4. Reaching blindly outward the hoary translucent apparition gained its footing.
   - a. a comma after the prepositional phrase
   - b. comma between adjectives preceding the noun
   - c. a comma after the participial phrase
   - d. a comma after the gerund phrase
   - e. an apostrophe in the contraction

5. Ola is the Spanish word for wave it is an easy noun to learn.
   - a. quotation marks around the Spanish noun
   - b. italics on the Spanish noun
   - c. a comma after the independent clause
   - d. a comma after the dependent clause
   - e. a semicolon after the independent clause

Answer Key

1. With a subtle sort of smile, the president said, "All citizens are created equal."
   a. a comma after the prepositional phrases   **d. quote marks around direct quotation**
   b. an apostrophe in the contraction   **e. period inside the closing quote marks**
   c. a comma before the direct quotation

   A comma after multiple introductory prepositional phrases. Our standard is to put the period inside the closing quotes, although corporations and the British often put it outside.

2. When the poet wrote *The Divine Comedy*, he created a new poetic form.
   a. a comma after the independent clause   **d. italics on the poem title**
   b. an apostrophe in the possessive noun   e. quotation marks around the poem title
   c. a comma after the dependent clause

   We need a D,I comma after the introductory dependent clause in this complex sentence, and with a poem as long and important as Dante's Divine Comedy, we should put the title in italics; after all, it makes an entire book.

3. A two-thirds Roman majority wanted circuses, bread, and gladiatorial entertainment.
   a. a hyphen in the compound adjective   **d. list comma before coordinating conj.**
   b. a colon at the beginning of the list   e. a comma after the dependent clause
   c. a comma after the plural common noun

   A hyphen makes two-thirds *a compound adjective, but if we said "it increased by two thirds," we wouldn't want the hyphen because then* thirds *would be a noun, and* two *would only be its modifying adjective. We prefer to put the list comma before the coordinating conjunction.*

4. Reaching blindly outward the hoary, grizzled apparition gained its footing.
   a. a comma after the prepositional phrase   d. a comma after the gerund phrase
   b. comma between adjectives preceding the noun e. an apostrophe in the contraction
   c. a comma after the participial phrase

   No comma after a single introductory prepositional phrase if no confusion is present. We separate multiple adjectives that precede and modify a noun—not including articles.

5. *Ola* is the Spanish word for *wave*; it is an easy noun to learn.
   a. quotation marks around the Spanish noun   d. a comma after the dependent clause
   b. italics on the Spanish noun   **e. semicolon after the independent clause**
   c. a comma after the independent clause

   We would actually put both Ola *and* wave *in italics; the first is a foreign language word and also a word as such, and the second is a word as such. We put an I;I semicolon between the two independent clauses in this compound sentence, since there is no coordinating conjunction between the clauses.*

Use the grammar clues to solve this Mystery Sentence:

This sentence from American history begins with a plural demonstrative pronoun, followed by a plural present tense linking verb, then a definite article, then a one-syllable plural common noun; this is followed by a relative clause beginning with a relative pronoun which is also sometimes a singular demonstrative pronoun, a plural present tense action verb, a possessive adjective based on the plural of the noun *man*, and a direct object made of a one-syllable plural common noun rhyming with *rolls*.

These are the times that try men's souls. - Thomas Paine

Identify the **part of speech** in **bold** in these sentences:

1. In the tropics the leafy **heliotropes** turn toward the sun.	noun
2. A gastrologist studies the stomach; a **gastronome** prepares food.	noun
3. The aged arthropod suffered **from** arthritis and arthralgia.	preposition
4. The popular ventriloquist had a heart operation on his **left** ventricle.	adjective
5. **Dorsiventral** leaves have distinct upper and lower surfaces.	adjective
6. The universe is sometimes referred to as the **macrocosm**.	noun
7. Are right-handed people really more **dexterous**?	adjective
8. **Brachypterous** insects have short wings.	adjective
9. **Brachiate** trees have widely spreading branches in pairs, like arms.	adjective
10. The branchiopods are marine crustaceans that breathe **through** gills.	preposition

Identify the **part of sentence** in **bold** in these sentences:

11. The hyperkinetic boy did not possess **telekinesis**, fortunately.	direct object
12. The species *Homo sapiens* **belongs** to the Chordata phylum.	predicate
13. **Reproduction** by budding is also called blastogenesis.	subject
14. If fingerprinting is dactylography, is sign language **dactylology**?	subject complement
15. If you press your closed **eyelids**, you will see phosphenes.	direct object
16. What **is** the difference between a pentagram and a pentagon?	predicate
17. Perlite is a volcanic **glass** that resembles obsidian.	subject complement
18. The voracious carnivore devoured the small **herbivore**.	direct object
19. The hologram gave the **scientists** a new view of the structure.	indirect object
20. The diploid **structure** divided into two haploid structures.	subject

Identify the type of **bold** phrase and give its part of speech:

1. Ishmael, **a member of the Anglican church**, is an Anglophile.   appositive, adjective

2. **To gain insight**, the anthropologist studies human cultures.   infinitive, adverb

3. **Resembling birds**, the pterosaur and pterodactyl were dinosaurs.   participial, adjective

4. Pithecanthropus skeletons were found **to be fragile**.   infinitive, adverb

5. Her calligraphy is ornate, like the music **of the calliope**.   prepositional, adjective

6. The austral winds raised storms **over the Australian outback**.   prepositional, adverb

7. **Trembling nervously**, a boy held the cephalopod in both hands.   participial, adjective

8. The physician asked the chiropractor **to practice chiromancy**.   infinitive, noun

9. The survivor **of the holocaust** made a caustic comment.   prepositional, adjective

10. **With a laugh**, the extraterrestrial admired the subterranean grottoes.   prepositional, adverb

Identify the **sentence structure** of each of these sentences. Disregard the bold.

11. The **cataract** and **cataclysm** caused **catastrophe** in the **catacombs**.   simple

12. The lying criminal **perjured** himself, but the **jury** listened.   compound

13. A **confluence** of **influences** made her **fluent** in Spanish, and it did.   compound

14. The senator's **adherents** laughed, and the speech was **incoherent**.   compound

15. The corrupt ruler was **deposed** when his **deposits** were discovered.   complex

16. His **mundane** conversation bored her to tears; it was too much.   compound

17. Is a **democracy** a **meritocracy** or a **plutocracy** for the **aristocracy**?   simple

18. **Egomania** kept him from noticing the **kleptomania** of his guest.   simple

19. Because he was **victimized** by his own ignorance, he paid a price.   complex

20. The **anthology** article discussed the **anthozoans**; it was good.   compound

For each of the following sentences, circle the letter of each answer that is true. The answer can be any combination, including all or none. This exercise will teach you the real process of punctuation as a function of grammar.

1. The Red River Valley is a nice tune to know when youre in the desert.
    a. italics on the song title
    b. quotation marks around the song title
    c. a comma after the dependent clause
    d. a comma after the independent clause
    e. an apostrophe in the contraction

2. Wow its fun to see three countries in a five day trip.
    a. a comma after the interjection
    b. an apostrophe in the possessive pronoun
    c. an apostrophe in the contraction
    d. a comma after the independent clauses
    e. a hyphen in the compound adjective

3. In the Jamestown colony the incidence of pneumonia was down by one third.
    a. comma after the introductory prepositional phrase
    b. a hyphen in the fraction
    c. a comma after the dependent clause
    d. commas around the appositive
    e. commas around the parenthetical remark

4. On December 4 1866 Wassily Kandinsky the abstract painter was born.
    a. a comma after the day
    b. a comma after the year appositive
    c. a comma after the participial phrase
    d. commas around the appositive
    e. a comma after the dependent clause

5. Caught by the swift current Dagoo gazed through the porthole.
    a. a comma after the dependent clause
    b. comma after the introductory prepositional phrases
    c. a comma after the participial phrase
    d. commas around the appositive
    e. a semicolon between the clauses

Answer Key

1. "The Red River Valley" is a nice tune to know when you're in the desert.
      a. italics on the song title   d. a comma after the independent clause
      b. quotation marks around the song title   **e. an apostrophe in the contraction**
      c. a comma after the dependent clause

   For the title of a song, a chapter, or an article, we use quotation marks; for the title of a book, an epic poem, or a major vessel of transport, we use italics. Remember that italics and underline are considered to be the same thing. On a typewriter, or when we are writing a research paper on the computer in `Courier type font,` *underline is better because Courier looks bad in italics. See:*

   I read *War and Peace* this week.
   `I read `*`War and Peace`*` this week.`
   `I read `<u>`War and Peace`</u>` this week.`

2. Wow, it's fun to see three countries in a five-day trip.
      a. a comma after the interjection   d. a comma after the independent clauses
      b. an apostrophe in the possessive pronoun   **e. a hyphen in the compound adjective**
      c. an apostrophe in the contraction

   It's is the contraction of it *and* is*; it needs an apostrophe.*

3. In the Jamestown colony the incidence of pneumonia was down by one third.
      a. comma after the introductory prepositional phrase   d. commas around the appositive
      b. a hyphen in the fraction   e. commas around the parenthetical remark
      c. a comma after the dependent clause

   No punctuation needed. Here the fraction is an adjective and a noun, rather than a compound adjective.

4. On December 4, 1866, Wassily Kandinsky, the abstract painter, was born.
      a. a comma after the day   **d. commas around the appositive**
      b. a comma after the year appositive   e. a comma after the dependent clause
      c. a comma after the participial phrase

   The sentence has two appositives, the year and then the definition of Kandinsky. Each one needs two commas to separate it from what it interrupts. The danger is always forgetting the second appositive comma.

5. Caught by the swift current, Dagoo gazed through the porthole.
      a. a comma after the dependent clause   d. commas around the appositive
      b. comma after the introductory prepositional phrases   e. a semicolon between the clauses
      c. a comma after the participial phrase

   We can't pick answer b because there is only one prepositional phrase at the beginning of the sentence, but it modifies a participle, so the answer is c.

Use the grammar clues to solve this Mystery Sentence:

This interrogative sentence from a children's nursery rhyme begins with a two-syllable proper noun, repeated twice and used as the noun of direct address, followed by an adverb modifying an adjective that rhymes with the first word of the sentence, then an interrogative adverb, a helping verb, a second person singular possessive pronoun, a two-syllable common noun, and a main verb.

Mary, Mary, quite contrary, how does your garden grow?

Identify the **part of speech** in **bold** in each sentence below:

1. The linguini-loving linguist knew the **lingua franca**.   noun

2. **Motile** microorganisms have powers of spontaneous motion.   adjective

3. The navy **circumnavigated** the globe by precise navigation.   verb

4. The **undulant** waves soon inundated the low regions.   adjective

5. The famous **polyglot** spoke seventeen languages.   noun

6. A hazy corona circled the moon the night **before** the coronation.   preposition

7. The goddess of the golden dawn, Aurora, held the **auriferous** rocks.   adjective

8. At the party the **literati** discussed the glories of literature.   noun

9. The rational person will not **rationalize** his wrongs away.   verb

10. Singing was an emotional **catharsis** for the vocalist.   noun

Identify the **part of sentence** in **bold** in each sentence below:

11. There **was** a disparity between his story and the facts.   predicate

12. Are the rewards of the job **commensurate** with the duties?   subject complement

13. We can choose either harmony or **acrimony**.   direct object

14. The quintet played **Mozart** to a group of quinquagenarians.   direct object

15. The **sociopath** used his knowledge of sociology to evil purposes.   subject

16. Ovoviviparous fish produce **eggs** that hatch inside the mother.   direct object

17. The **dysphasia** resulted from injury to the brain's speech center.   subject

18. His resignation **obviated** the need for impeachment proceedings.   predicate

19. Are you studying these phenomena or this **phenomenon**?   direct object

20. Histology is the **study** of the structure of plant and animal tissues. subject complement

For each sentence, identify the type of **bold** phrase and its part of speech:

1. The atmometer measures the rate **of evaporation** of water.   prepositional, adjective

2. **Completely fascinated**, the cardiologist saw the electrocardiogram.   participial, adjective

3. **For a technician**, the Soviet cosmonaut had cosmopolitan tastes.   prepositional, adverb

4. The order **to attack quickly** was countermanded by his counterpart.   infinitive, adjective

5. The craniotomy was performed **by a skilled brain surgeon**.   prepositional, adverb

6. As if **to make a point**, the cyclone hurled the bicycle fifty yards.   infinitive, adverb

7. Agnostics are not usually attracted **to Gnosticism**.   prepositional, adverb

8. Over the years, his habits had ossified **beyond hope of change**.   prepositional, adverb

9. Beetles, **xylophagous insects**, had eaten the antique xylophone.   appositive, adjective

10. The costermonger and fishmonger shouted out prices **to passersby**.   prepositional, adverb

For each sentence, identify the **sentence structure**. Disregard bold type.

11. **September** was the seventh month of the Roman calendar.   simple

12. I know; the flood of immigration stirred the public **xenophobia**.   compound

13. The **cardiovascular** system responded as the exercise increased.   complex

14. The storm **forecast** filled her with **foreboding**, but it was not enough.   compound

15. When she looked, the **smallish** object had a faint, **greenish** tint.   complex

16. Their assault on the summit was **hopeless**, **bootless**, and **fruitless**.   simple

17. As you know, we think high fashion is a **barometer** for new trends.   complex

18. The geologist studied the **ferrous** rock with care, but he missed it.   compound

19. The **quasi-military** operation into Cambodia has failed; it is true.   compound

20. We visited **Polynesia**, **Micronesia**, and **Melanesia** and came home.   simple

For each of the following sentences, circle the letter of each answer that is true. The answer can be any combination, including all or none. This exercise will teach you the real process of punctuation as a function of grammar.

1. In December Baltimore lost its best player when a bizarre event occurred.

    a. a comma after the prepositional phrase

    b. a comma after the month

    c. an apostrophe in the possessive pronoun

    d. an apostrophe in the contraction

    e. a comma between the clauses

2. Because the wind was roaring we remained on the beach.

    a. a comma after the participial phrase

    b. a comma after the dependent clause

    c. a comma after the independent clause

    d. a semicolon between the clauses

    e. a comma after the prepositional phrase

3. The well intentioned athlete ran two miles uphill one downhill and one level.

    a. a hyphen in the compound adjective

    b. a colon before the list

    c. a comma after the adjective uphill

    d. a list comma after the adjective downhill

    e. a comma between the clauses

4. Flying across the Pacific was Noonans greatest dream.

    a. a comma after the introductory participial phrase

    b. a comma after the dependent clause

    c. an apostrophe in the possessive noun

    d. commas around the appositive phrase

    e. commas around the parenthetical remark

5. Yes the English lost twenty five fighters in the Battle of Britain.

    a. a comma after the introductory adverb

    b. a comma after the interjection

    c. a comma after the dependent clause

    d. a hyphen in the compound adjective

    e. a comma before the prepositional phrase

Answer Key

1. In December Baltimore lost its best player when a bizarre event occurred.
   a. a comma after the prepositional phrase
   b. a comma after the month
   c. an apostrophe in the possessive pronoun
   d. an apostrophe in the contraction
   e. a comma between the clauses

   No punctuation needed; this is a complex sentence with an ID clause structure. If it read the other way around: "When a bizarre event occurred, Baltimore lost its best player," then it would be a D,I structure and would need the comma.

2. Because the wind was roaring we remained on the beach.
   a. a comma after the participial phrase
   b. a comma after the dependent clause
   c. a comma after the independent clause
   d. a semicolon between the clauses
   e. a comma after the prepositional phrase

   This is a D,I complex sentence that begins with a subordinating conjunction to introduce the dependent clause.

3. The well-intentioned athlete ran two miles uphill, one downhill, and one level.
   a. a hyphen in the compound adjective
   b. a colon before the list
   c. a comma after **uphill**
   d. a list comma after **downhill**
   e. a comma between the clauses

   Again, though some style manuals will now abandon the list comma before the coordinating conjunction, we feel it best to retain it.

4. Flying across the Pacific was Noonan's greatest dream.
   a. a comma after the introductory participial phrase
   b. a comma after the dependent clause
   c. an apostrophe in the possessive noun
   d. commas around the appositive phrase
   e. commas around the parenthetical remark

   Even though this sentence begins with a gerund phrase (which contains a prepositional phrase), we will not put a comma after it because it is the subject of the sentence, and we do not separate the subject from its predicate.

5. Yes, the English lost twenty-five fighters in the Battle of Britain.
   a. a comma after the introductory adverb
   b. a comma after the interjection
   c. a comma after the dependent clause
   d. a hyphen in the compound adjective
   e. a comma before the prepositional phrase

   An interjection, since it has no grammatical function, is not connected to anything, so it can be separated with a comma without doing violence to the kinds of relationships that other parts of speech have.

Use the grammar clues to solve this Mystery Sentence:

A famous sentence from Shakespeare begins with a compound infinitive in which the second infinitive in the compound is negated by an adverb and ends with a clause that contains a demonstrative pronoun as a subject, a present tense linking verb, a definite article, and a singular common noun as a subject complement.

To be or not to be, that is the question. (Hamlet)

For each sentence, identify the **part of speech** of the word in **bold**.

1. We **convened** at the Hilton on Third Avenue.   verb

2. The **ichthyologist** removed the petrified ichthyosaur bones.   noun

3. The **gravamen** of the charges is that he left his post under fire.   noun

4. The calorimeter measured the heat of the **calorific** reaction.   adjective

5. **Heliophiles** catch few solar rays at the winter solstice.   noun

6. The ophthalmologist treats the diseases of **the** eye.   adjective

7. There were nucleotides in the chromosomes **of** the cell nucleus.   preposition

8. He tried **to sate** his insatiable appetite for pizza.   noun

9. Male proterandrous insects appear earlier in the season **than** females. conjunction

10. The montane vistas of Montevideo **are** like those in Montana.   verb

For each sentence, identify the **part of sentence** of the word in **bold**.

11. A kilometer, one thousand meters, is 0.62137 **miles** in length.   subject complement

12. Myriad **explanations** exist of unidentified flying objects.   subject

13. At the first sign of tachycardia, he **was rushed** to the hospital.   predicate

14. Is nuclear fission the **opposite** of nuclear fusion?   subject complement

15. The cumulus clouds accumulated as the sun baked the **sea**.   direct object

16. The meteorologist reported that the meteorite did no **damage**.   direct object

17. The hibernal winds did not reach the hibernating **bear**.   direct object

18. The dilemma **was** whether to study the dicotyledon or diencephalon.   predicate

19. The **bathymetry** of the Pacific was easily studied with a bathyscaph. subject

20. Barnacles and other cirripeds covered the marina's **pilings**.   direct object

For each sentence, identify the type of **phrase** in **bold**.

1.	The gloomy soul was unable **to overcome her melancholy**.	infinitive, adverb
2.	**Suddenly stumbling**, the vice president greeted the vice consul.	participial, adjective
3.	Agent Orange was a toxic defoliant used **in the Vietnam War**.	prepositional, adverb
4.	**To provide relief**, we filled the atomizer with a new scent.	infinitive, adverb
5.	**In morphological terms**, orbicular leaves are circular and flat.	prepositional, adverb
6.	Her multifarious nefarious deeds landed her **in prison**.	prepositional, adverb
7.	The ignis fatuus seemed to ignite and hover **over the swamp**.	prepositional, adverb
8.	We could do nothing **to mollify the man's anger**.	infinitive, adjective
9.	Quickly delineate your proposal **for the new rapid transit system**.	prepositional, adjective
10.	Hemiplegia, **a partial paralysis**, is a serious condition.	appositive, adjective

For each sentence, identify the **sentence structure**. Disregard the bold.

11.	The obsessed **oologist** painted his house; it was robin's-egg blue.	compound
12.	As we became aware of the ship's **retrograde** motion, we sank.	complex
13.	The **pneumococcus** bacteria gave him **pneumonia**, and it was bad.	compound
14.	Skeletons of the microscopic **radiolarians** show **radial** symmetry.	simple
15.	The sponge expels water through its **osculum**; this is well known.	compound
16.	As you saw, the **immense** wall was **impervious** to cannon fire.	complex
17.	The **convection** current distributed the heat of the flames.	simple
18.	Houdini accomplished feats of **prestidigitation**, but he was doomed.	compound
19.	The **gymnasium** is the perfect place for **gymnastics**, or so I think.	compound
20.	An Amoeba's **cytoplasm** includes **endoplasm** and **ectoplasm**.	simple

For each of the following sentences, circle the letter of each answer that is true. The answer can be any combination, including all or none. This exercise will teach you the real process of punctuation as a function of grammar.

1. The Neotitanic the fastest cruise ship on the planet can reach fifty two knots.

    a. quotation marks around the ship title
    b. italics on the ship title
    c. commas around the dependent clause

    d. commas around the appositive
    e. a hyphen in the compound number

2. Taken by surprise the yellow spider jumped at the arachnologist.

    a. a comma after the dependent clause
    b. a comma after the gerund phrase
    c. a comma after the participial phrase

    d. commas around the appositive
    e. quotation marks around the subject

3. The new usher who happens to have the letter m on his cap is short.

    a. a comma after the compound subject
    b. commas around the appositive
    c. commas around the nonessential clause

    d. a semicolon between the independent clauses
    e. italics on the letter as such

4. The Virginia colony needed three things salt pepper and catsup.

    a. a semicolon between the clauses
    b. a colon after the plural noun
    c. a comma after **salt**

    d. a list comma before the coordinating conjunction
    e. commas around the parenthetical remark

5. Did you read the story Digital Literature in this months Electrica Magazine?

    a. quotation marks around the story title
    b. italics on the story title
    c. commas around the appositive

    d. italics on the magazine title
    e. an apostrophe in the possessive noun

Answer Key

1. The *Neotitanic*, the fastest cruise ship on the planet, can reach fifty-two knots.
   a. quotation marks around the ship title
   b. italics on the ship title
   c. commas around the dependent clause
   d. commas around the appositive
   e. a hyphen in the compound number

   Remember to put two commas around an appositive. This sentence is a good example of the confusion that can happen if you forget the second appositive comma.

2. Taken by surprise, the yellow spider jumped at the arachnologist.
   a. a comma after the dependent clause
   b. a comma after the gerund phrase
   c. a comma after the participial phrase
   d. commas around the appositive
   e. quotation marks around the subject

   A comma goes after an introductory participial phrase, meaning, one that introduces a sentence.

3. The new usher, who happens to have the letter *m* on his cap, is short.
   a. a comma after the compound subject
   b. commas around the appositive
   c. commas around the nonessential clause
   d. a semicolon between the independent clauses
   e. italics on the letter as such

   You can tell by the wording that this clause is not essential to the sentence, but is just extra information. It is optional, and is an interruption. That is why it gets commas around it. We always put words, letters, and numbers as such in italics.

4. The Virginia colony needed three things: salt, pepper, and catsup.
   a. a semicolon between the clauses
   b. a colon after the plural noun
   c. a comma after salt
   d. list comma before coordinating conj.
   e. commas around the parenthetical remark

   Here we need the colon because the list follows and explains the direct object. If it read "The Virginia colony needed salt, pepper, and catsup," then we would not need the colon because the list would just be a compound direct object, and we never want to put a comma between the action verb and the direct object!

5. Did you read the story, "Digital Literature," in this month's *Electrica Magazine*?
   a. quotation marks around the story title
   b. italics on the story title
   c. commas around the appositive
   d. italics on the magazine title
   e. an apostrophe in the possessive noun

   Articles are in quotes, magazine titles are in italics.

Every planet has a magnetic field around it.

1. The word **every** is
   a. an adverb
   (b.) an adjective
   c. a preposition
   (d.) a conjunction

2. The word **planet** is
   (a.) a noun
   b. a pronoun
   c. an adjective
   d. an adverb

3. The word **magnetic**
   a. is a verb
   (b.) modifies **field**
   c. modifies **planet**
   d. is an adverb

4. The word **around** is
   a. a conjunction
   (b.) a preposition
   c. an adverb
   d. a pronoun

5. The word **it** is
   a. a noun and a subject
   b. an object of preposition
   c. a pronoun and a subject
   (d.) a pronoun

6. The sentence purpose is
   (a.) declarative
   b. interrogative
   c. imperative
   d. exclamatory

7. The sentence structure is
   (a.) simple
   b. compound
   c. complex
   d. compound-complex

8. The sentence subject is
   a. Every
   (b.) planet
   c. magnetic
   d. field

9. The verb/predicate is
   a. magnetic
   b. field
   c. around
   (d.) has

10. The verb is
    a. action and present tense
    b. action and past tense
    (c.) linking and present tense
    d. linking and past tense

The Martian visitors will have landed by Thursday.

11. The subject is
    a. Martian
    b. visitors
    c. Thursday
    d. landed

12. The sentence contains
    a. one preposition
    b. two prepositions
    c. three prepositions
    d. no prepositions

13. The word **Martian** is
    a. a proper noun
    b. a proper adjective
    c. a common noun
    d. a common adjective

14. The word **Thursday** is
    a. an adjective
    b. a noun
    c. a pronoun
    d. an interjection

15. The sentence contains
    a. one verb
    b. two verbs
    c. three verbs
    d. four verbs

16. The sentence contains
    a. one article
    b. two articles
    c. an infinitive
    d. none of the above

17. The phrase **by Thursday** modifies
    a. Martian
    b. visitors
    c. will have landed
    d. none of the above

18. The verb tense is
    a. present tense
    b. past
    c. future
    d. future perfect

19. The sentence purpose is
    a. declarative
    b. interrogative
    c. imperative
    d. exclamatory

20. The sentence structure is
    a. simple
    b. compound
    c. complex
    d. compound-complex

The Andromedans attacked savagely, and we fell back.

21. The word **we** is
    a. a noun
    b. a pronoun
    c. an adjective
    d. a verb

22. The word **savagely** is
    a. an adjective
    b. a verb
    c. an adverb
    d. a preposition

23. The word **Andromedans** is
    a. a common noun
    b. a proper noun
    c. a proper adjective
    d. a common adjective

24. The verbs are
    a. present tense
    b. past tense
    c. future tense
    d. past perfect tense

25. The word **and** is
    a. a subordinating conjunction
    b. a coordinating conjunction
    c. a correlative conjunction
    d. none of the above

26. The sentence contains
    a. one clause
    b. two clauses
    c. three clauses
    d. four clauses

27. The sentence contains
    a. no preposition
    b. one prepositions
    c. two prepositions
    d. three prepositions

28. The word **back** is
    a. a verb
    b. an adverb
    c. a preposition
    d. an adjective

29. The sentence purpose is
    a. declarative
    b. imperative
    c. exclamatory
    d. interrogative

30. The sentence structure is
    a. simple
    b. compound
    c. complex
    d. compound-complex

Explosions and cataclysms rocked the night thunderously.

31. The word **rocked** is
    a. a verb
    b. a past tense verb
    c. a past tense action verb
    d. none of the above

32. The word **thunderously** is
    a. an adjective
    b. an adverb
    c. a verb
    d. a preposition

33. The sentence contains
    a. no prepositional phrase
    b. one prepositional phrase
    c. two prepositional phrases
    d. three prepositional phrases

34. The word **Explosions** is
    a. a noun
    b. a pronoun
    c. a proper noun
    d. a common, plural noun

35. The word **and** is
    a. a subordinating conjunction
    b. a coordinating conjunction
    c. a correlative conjunction
    d. not a conjunction

36. The verb in the sentence is
    a. singular
    b. plural
    c. singular and past tense
    d. plural and past tense

37. The subject of the sentence is
    a. singular
    b. plural
    c. there is no subject
    d. none of the above

38. The sentence structure is
    a. simple
    b. compound
    c. complex
    d. compound-complex

39. The sentence contains
    a. one adjective
    b. two adjectives
    c. three adjectives
    d. no adjective

40. The sentence contains
    a. no gerund
    b. one gerund
    c. two gerunds
    d. three gerunds

Our ship was hit by a weaker beam.

41. The subject is
    a. ship
    b. our
    c. hit
    d. beam

42. The word **by** is
    a. an adverb
    b. a conjunction
    c. a preposition
    d. a verb

43. The word **beam** is
    a. a noun
    b. a pronoun
    c. a verb
    d. an interjection

44. The verb is
    a. was
    b. hit
    c. both a and b
    d. none of the above

45. The adjective **weaker** is in the
    a. positive degree
    b. comparative degree
    c. superlative degree
    d. none of the above

46. The sentence purpose is
    a. declarative
    b. imperative
    c. interrogative
    d. exclamatory

47. The verb in the sentence is
    a. active voice
    b. passive voice
    c. linking
    d. transitive

48. The sentence contains
    a. one gerund
    b. one participle
    c. one infinitive
    d. no verbal

49. The sentence is
    a. simple
    b. compound
    c. complex
    d. compound-complex

50. The subject of the sentence is
    a. singular
    b. plural
    c. there is no way to tell
    d. none of the above

Every planet has a magnetic field around it.

1. The word **every** is
   a. an adverb
   b. an adjective
   c. a preposition
   d. a conjunction

2. The word **planet** is
   a. a noun
   b. a pronoun
   c. an adjective
   d. an adverb

3. The word **magnetic**
   a. is a verb
   b. modifies field
   c. modifies planet
   d. is an adverb

4. The word **around** is
   a. a conjunction
   b. a preposition
   c. an adverb
   d. a pronoun

5. The word **it** is
   a. a noun and a subject
   b. an object of preposition
   c. a pronoun and a subject
   d. a pronoun

6. The sentence purpose is
   a. declarative
   b. interrogative
   c. imperative
   d. exclamatory

7. The sentence structure is
   a. simple
   b. compound
   c. complex
   d. compound-complex

8. The sentence subject is
   a. Every
   b. planet
   c. magnetic
   d. field

9. The verb/predicate is
   a. magnetic
   b. field
   c. around
   d. has

10. The verb is
    a. action and present tense
    b. action and past tense
    c. linking and present tense
    d. linking and past tense

The Martian visitors will have landed by Thursday.

11. The subject is
    a. Martian
    b. visitors
    c. Thursday
    d. landed

12. The sentence contains
    a. one preposition
    b. two prepositions
    c. three prepositions
    d. no prepositions

13. The word **Martian** is
    a. a proper noun
    b. a proper adjective
    c. a common noun
    d. a common adjective

14. The word **Thursday** is
    a. an adjective
    b. a noun
    c. a pronoun
    d. an interjection

15. The sentence contains
    a. one verb
    b. two verbs
    c. three verbs
    d. four verbs

16. The sentence contains
    a. one article
    b. two articles
    c. an infinitive
    d. none of the above

17. The phrase **by Thursday** modifies
    a. Martian
    b. visitors
    c. will have landed
    d. none of the above

18. The verb tense is
    a. present tense
    b. past
    c. future
    d. future perfect

19. The sentence purpose is
    a. declarative
    b. interrogative
    c. imperative
    d. exclamatory

20. The sentence structure is
    a. simple
    b. compound
    c. complex
    d. compound-complex

The Andromedans attacked savagely, and we fell back.

21. The word **we** is
    a. a noun
    b. a pronoun
    c. an adjective
    d. a verb

22. The word **savagely** is
    a. an adjective
    b. a verb
    c. an adverb
    d. a preposition

23. The word **Andromedans** is
    a. a common noun
    b. a proper noun
    c. a proper adjective
    d. a common adjective

24. The verbs are
    a. present tense
    b. past tense
    c. future tense
    d. past perfect tense

25. The word **and** is
    a. a subordinating conjunction
    b. a coordinating conjunction
    c. a correlative conjunction
    d. none of the above

26. The sentence contains
    a. one clause
    b. two clauses
    c. three clauses
    d. four clauses

27. The sentence contains
    a. no preposition
    b. one prepositions
    c. two prepositions
    d. three prepositions

28. The word **back** is
    a. a verb
    b. an adverb
    c. a preposition
    d. an adjective

29. The sentence purpose is
    a. declarative
    b. imperative
    c. exclamatory
    d. interrogative

30. The sentence structure is
    a. simple
    b. compound
    c. complex
    d. compound-complex

Explosions and cataclysms rocked the night thunderously.

31. The word **rocked** is
    a. a verb
    b. a past tense verb
    c. a past tense action verb
    d. none of the above

32. The word **thunderously** is
    a. an adjective
    b. an adverb
    c. a verb
    d. a preposition

33. The sentence contains
    a. no prepositional phrase
    b. one prepositional phrase
    c. two prepositional phrases
    d. three prepositional phrases

34. The word **Explosions** is
    a. a noun
    b. a pronoun
    c. a proper noun
    d. a common, plural noun

35. The word **and** is
    a. a subordinating conjunction
    b. a coordinating conjunction
    c. a correlative conjunction
    d. not a conjunction

36. The verb in the sentence is
    a. singular
    b. plural
    c. singular and past tense
    d. plural and past tense

37. The subject of the sentence is
    a. singular
    b. plural
    c. there is no subject
    d. none of the above

38. The sentence structure is
    a. simple
    b. compound
    c. complex
    d. compound-complex

39. The sentence contains
    a. one adjective
    b. two adjectives
    c. three adjectives
    d. no adjectives

40. The sentence contains
    a. no gerund
    b. one gerund
    c. two gerunds
    d. three gerunds

Our ship was hit by a weaker beam.

41. The subject is
    a. ship
    b. our
    c. hit
    d. beam

42. The word **by** is
    a. an adverb
    b. a conjunction
    c. a preposition
    d. a verb

43. The word **beam** is
    a. a noun
    b. a pronoun
    c. a verb
    d. an interjection

44. The verb is
    a. was
    b. hit
    c. both a and b
    d. none of the above

45. The adjective **weaker** is in the
    a. positive degree
    b. comparative degree
    c. superlative degree
    d. none of the above

46. The sentence purpose is
    a. declarative
    b. imperative
    c. interrogative
    d. exclamatory

47. The verb in the sentence is
    a. active voice
    b. passive voice
    c. linking
    d. transitive

48. The sentence contains
    a. one gerund
    b. one participle
    c. one infinitive
    d. no verbal

49. The sentence is
    a. simple
    b. compound
    c. complex
    d. compound-complex

50 The subject of the sentence is
    a. singular
    b. plural
    c. there is no way to tell
    d. none of the above

Use the grammar clues to solve this Mystery Sentence:

A sentence from a lullaby begins with a four-word dependent clause containing a subordinating conjunction, a definite article, a singular common noun, and an intransitive present tense action verb. This is followed by an independent clause containing a definite article, a singular common noun, and a future tense intransitive action verb.

When the wind blows, the cradle will rock.

Identify the **part of speech** in **bold** in each sentence below:

1.   The **equivocating** politician praised both groups.   adjective

2.   A **superfluous** comment is a waste of time.   adjective

3.   The two nations formed a **bilateral** agreement.   adjective

4.   A **circumspect** reply is safer.   adjective

5.   A big job needs a **commensurate** reward.   adjective

6.   The creature cast a **malevolent** glare.   adjective

7.   She is a **neophyte** in the art world.   noun

8.   The grouchy **misanthropist** wouldn't contribute.   noun

9.   The **bellicose** tribe attacked without warning.   adjective

10.   They believe in an **anthropomorphic** god.   adjective

Identify the *part of sentence* in *italics* in each sentence below:

11.   The **captious** *remarks* were not sincere.   subject

12.   Create a **neologism**, like "televoracious."   direct object

13.   The convict's muttered **malediction** was *inaudible*.   subject complement

14.   Her **incredulous** expression showed her *feelings*.   direct object

15.   You can't keep *secrets* from an **omniscient** god.   direct object

16.   It was a *hobby* that became a **monomania**.   subject complement

17.   You have a convincing but unfortunately **specious** *argument*.   direct object

18.   His speech **excoriated** the *opponent*.   direct object

19.   We saw an early **prototype** of the Mustang.   direct object

20.   It is a hostile, **xenophobic** *country*.   subject complement

For each sentence, identify the type of *phrase* in *italics* and its part of speech:

1.	It can be difficult *to **mollify** someone's anger.*	infinitive, adverb
2.	*Up the bank* splashed a water-logged **ichthyologist**.	prepositional, adverb
3.	*Speaking seven languages,* she is a brilliant **polyglot**.	participial, adjective
4.	Look *through the **diaphanous** draperies.*	prepositional, adverb
5.	*The **somniferous** speaking* put him to sleep.	gerund, noun
6.	He has a comfortable **sinecure** *in his uncle's firm.*	prepositional, adverb
7.	*For modern critics,* Hamlet's famous **soliloquy** is the question.	prepositional, adverb
8.	The **adherents** *of a militaristic foreign policy* want war.	prepositional, adjective
9.	***To abjure** one's former beliefs* is stressful.	infinitive, noun
10.	The **caustic** comments *about her clothes* hurt her.	prepositional, adjective

For each sentence, identify the **sentence structure**. Disregard bold type.

11.	The idea was formed by a **confluence** of other ideas.	simple
12.	He was **deposed** without violence; everyone approved.	compound
13.	The offensive **egomaniac** praised himself as we expected.	complex
14.	When it happened, it was **egregious** act of vandalism.	complex
15.	Take an extra-strength **analgesic** for the headache, and sleep.	compound
16.	Try to divine the future through superannuated **chiromancy**.	simple
17.	The corrupt **oligarchy** kept control when the revolution failed.	complex
18.	The bigot's **intractable** opinions were unchangeable.	simple
19.	The **intransigent** true believers wouldn't budge; I know.	compound
20.	When night fell, his **perfidious** cowardice made him infamous.	complex

For each of the following sentences, circle the letter of each answer that is true. The answer can be any combination, including all or none. This exercise will teach you the real process of punctuation as a function of grammar.

1. In the thriving Delaware colony the heavy market in iron tools was raising profits.

    a. comma after the introductory prepositional phrase
    b. a comma after the dependent clause
    c. commas around the parenthetical remark
    d. a semicolon between the independent clauses
    e. a hyphen in the compound adjective

2. The insects that ate the wooden braces are hard to eliminate.

    a. commas around the appositive
    b. a semicolon between the independent clauses
    c. commas around the nonessential clause
    d. quotation marks around the word **braces**
    e. a comma before the infinitive

3. Robert Dubious our new senator was opposed however its happening.

    a. commas around the appositive
    b. a semicolon between the independent clauses
    c. a comma after **however**
    d. an apostrophe in the contraction
    e. a comma after the dependent clause

4. In the winter of 76 the wolfs teeth left marks like letter vs on the windowsill.

    a. an apostrophe before the contraction
    b. comma after the introductory prepositional phrases
    c. an apostrophe in the possessive noun
    d. italics on the letter as such
    e. an apostrophe in the plural letter as such

5. The heavily loaded jeep careened across the plain.

    a. comma between adjectives preceding the subject
    b. a comma after the independent clause
    c. a semicolon between the independent clauses
    d. a comma before the prepositional phrases
    e. a comma before the participial phrase

Answer Key

1. In the thriving Delaware colony, the heavy market in iron tools was raising profits.
   a. comma after the introductory prep. phrase   d. a semicolon between the independent clauses
   b. a comma after the dependent clause   e. a hyphen in the compound adjective
   c. commas around the parenthetical remark

   This introductory prepositional phrase is long enough to merit a comma; when these introductory phrases get wordy enough, we want to make sure they don't get mixed up with the subject of the sentence.

2. The insects that ate the wooden braces are hard to eliminate.
   a. commas around the appositive   d. quotation marks around the word **braces**
   b. a semicolon between the independent clauses   e. a comma before the infinitive
   c. commas around the nonessential clause

   This sentence contains an adjective clause modifying the subject, but the question is, is the adjective clause essential or nonessential? We have to decide because if it is nonessential, we have to put commas around it. The best answer here is that the clause is essential; it tells which insects, and is not just an unnecessary interruption. Therefore, we do not need commas, because it is important and needs to be there.

3. Robert Dubious, our new senator, was opposed; however, it's happening.
   a. commas around the appositive   **d. an apostrophe in the contraction**
   b. a semicolon between the independent clauses   e. a comma after the dependent clause
   c. a comma after *however*

   This illustrates the correct treatment of a compound sentence in which the second clause begins with the word however.

4. In the winter of '76, the wolf's teeth left marks like letter *v*'s on the windowsill.
   a. an apostrophe before the contraction   **d. italics on the letter as such**
   b. comma after the introductory prep. phrases   **e. apostrophe in the plural letter as such**
   c. an apostrophe in the possessive noun

   Lots of action in this sentence. Remember that letters, numbers, and words as such are always in italics (or underlined). If you mean the word dog, *rather than the four-footed kind, you italicize* dog. *In this sentence, which is all in italics, I do just the reverse, and it means the same thing.*

5. The heavily loaded jeep careened across the plain.
   a. comma between adjectives preceding the subject   d. a comma before the prepositional phrases
   b. a comma after the independent clause   e. a comma before the participial phrase
   c. a semicolon between the independent clauses

   No punctuation.

Use the grammar clues to solve this Mystery Sentence:

A four-word simple declarative sentence is one of the most famous statements made by an American civil rights leader. The sentence begins with its subject, a first person singular personal pronoun. The next word is a present tense action verb, which happens to be a word which is often used as a helping verb in the perfect tenses. The sentence concludes with an indefinite article and a subject complement, a singular common noun.

I have a dream. (Martin Luther King)

Identify the **part of speech** in **bold** in each sentence below:

1.	The **egocentric** snob didn't notice who he hurt.	adjective
2.	A paycheck is one of the **tangible** benefits of a job.	adjective
3.	The **demagogue** played on public prejudices.	noun
4.	Don't **preclude** that option.	verb
5.	British **cryptologists** cracked the German code.	noun
6.	We deplore his narrow **ethnocentrism**.	noun
7.	A humorless pedant is a poor **pedagogue**.	noun
8.	Galileo was forced **to recant** his heliocentric statements.	adverb
9.	Permission to travel has been **revoked**.	verb
10.	The **pugnacious** bully got his comeuppance.	adjective

Identify the *part of sentence* in *italics* in each sentence below:

11.	Her **incisive** *questions* cut deeply into the issue.	subject
12.	The German leader delivered a *diatribe* against France.	direct object
13.	There is an inexplicable *anomaly* in the data.	subject complement
14.	Please **enumerate** your *reasons*.	direct object
15.	You must *choose* among certain **circumscribed** alternatives.	predicate
16.	We are *forced* **to intercede** on behalf of the orphan.	predicate
17.	The **disputatious** reporter irritated the *official*.	direct object
18.	The **loquacious** fellow wore their *ears* out.	direct object
19.	We **abrogate** an *agreement* only out of dire necessity.	direct object
20.	A **prescient** *vision* came to him in a dream.	subject

For each sentence, identify the type of *italics phrase* and give its part of speech:

1.	It is time **to advocate** *a new policy.*	infinitive, adjective
2.	He was crushed by the **ponderous** burden *of the decision.*	prepositional, adjective
3.	*Living in fear*, the Gauls expected a brutal **retribution**.	participial, adjective
4.	The **android's** metallic eye glistened *from across the room.*	prepositional, adverb
5.	The crusade *against the infidels* was unsuccessful.	prepositional, adjective
6.	The **resurgence** *of patriotism* began slowly.	prepositional, adjective
7.	She, *a conventional person*, liked his **punctilious** formal conduct.	appositive, adjective
8.	His **condescending** attitude was infuriating *to all of us.*	prepositional, adverb
9.	The two **collateral** issues could not be discussed *at one time.*	prepositional, adverb
10.	The past, *an eternal mystery*, is **irrevocable** and answers no call.	appositive, adjective

For each sentence, identify the **sentence structure**. Disregard bold type.

11.	Please **elucidate** the matter for our less enlightened guest.	simple
12.	Franklin's witty **epigrams** amuse us; we still read them.	compound
13.	As time went on, his **eccentric** personality began to moderate.	complex
14.	It is wise to be **cognizant** of the laws regulating investments.	simple
15.	As I mentioned, the **stringent** regulations seemed severe.	complex
16.	The **anthropoid** apes have recognizable facial expressions.	simple
17.	Her **diffident** glance caught his eye when she looked up.	complex
18.	**Pandemonium** erupted on the playground; it was fun.	compound
19.	The diplomat's **urbane** manners set the tone since they left.	complex
20.	Because of his spirit, the **tractable** boy was a pleasure to know.	simple

For each of the following sentences, circle the letter of each answer that is true. The answer can be any combination, including all or none. This exercise will teach you the real process of punctuation as a function of grammar.

1. In April she returned and the organization recovered its profits.
   a. a comma after the prepositional phrase
   b. a comma after the dependent clause
   c. a comma after the independent clause
   d. an apostrophe in the contraction
   e. commas before and after the appositive

2. Near Boston Massachusetts the whales avoided Ahabs ship.
   a. a comma after the city
   b. a comma after the state appositive
   c. an apostrophe in the plural noun
   d. an apostrophe in the possessive noun
   e. a comma after the dependent clause

3. A better feeling arose when Stubb the experienced officer walked forward.
   a. a comma to separate the adjectives preceding the noun
   b. a comma before the dependent clause
   c. a comma after the independent clause
   d. commas around the appositive
   e. commas around the noun of direct address

4. Melvilles novel Moby Dick contains a ship named The Pequod.
   a. italics on the ship title
   b. an apostrophe in the possessive noun
   c. quotation marks around the book title
   d. italics on the book title
   e. commas around the appositive

5. The well intentioned remark and the reaction caused thirty five resignations.
   a. a comma between the modifiers that precede the noun.
   b. a hyphen in the compound adjective preceding the noun.
   c. a comma after the dependent clause
   d. a hyphen in the compound number
   e. an apostrophe in the possessive noun

For each of the following sentences, circle the letter of each answer that is true. The answer can be any combination, including all or none. This exercise will teach you the real process of punctuation as a function of grammar.

1. In April she returned, and the organization recovered its profits.
   a. a comma after the prepositional phrase
   b. a comma after the dependent clause
   c. a comma after the independent clause
   d. an apostrophe in the contraction
   e. commas before and after the appositive

   There is no contraction in the sentence; its is a possessive pronoun, which does not use an apostrophe since it is already possessive. No comma needed after the single, short prepositional phrase.

2. Near Boston, Massachusetts, the whales avoided Ahab's ship.
   a. a comma after the city
   b. a comma after the state appositive
   c. an apostrophe in the plural noun
   d. an apostrophe in the possessive noun
   e. a comma after the dependent clause

   The state appositive should be set off by commas before and after.

3. A better feeling arose when Stubb, the experienced officer, walked forward.
   a. a comma to separate the adjectives preceding the noun
   b. a comma before the dependent clause
   c. a comma after the independent clause
   d. commas around the appositive
   e. commas around the noun of direct address

   Appositives usually take two commas, since they typically interrupt sentences in order to define.

4. Melville's novel, *Moby Dick,* contains a ship named *The Pequod.*
   a. italics on the ship title
   b. an apostrophe in the possessive noun
   c. quotation marks around the book title
   d. italics on the book title
   e. commas around the appositive

   Novel titles and great vessel titles are in italics. If we did not put the two appositive commas in, some brief confusion might arise in the reading of the sentence.

5. The well intentioned remark and the reaction caused thirty five resignations.
   a. a comma between the modifiers that precede the noun.
   b. hyphen in compound adj. preceding noun.
   c. a comma after the dependent clause
   d. a hyphen in the compound number
   e. an apostrophe in the possessive noun

   The hyphen between well *and* intentioned *unites the two words into a single, modifying unity.*

Use the grammar clues to solve this Mystery Sentence:

One of the most famous sentences from the history of warfare in the United States is a simple declarative sentence which begins with a first person singular personal pronoun, then contains a verb phrase in which the verb, which is the first person singular present perfect tense of the verb *to begin*, is separated from its helping verb by two adverbs, then concludes with an infinitive.

I have not yet begun to fight. (John Paul Jones)

Identify the **part of speech** in **bold** in each sentence below:

1.	The quiet boy is an **introspective** loner.	adjective
2.	We should not **intervene** in their dispute	verb
3.	Down's **syndrome** has well-known symptoms.	noun
4.	He resented his **subordinate** rank in the military.	adjective
5.	A **dissonant** clamor arose in the streets.	adjective
6.	The **belligerent** nations refused to negotiate.	adjective
7.	It takes money to become a **credible** candidate.	adjective
8.	"The shadow of **impending** doom" is a trite phrase.	adjective
9.	Bach's **polyphonic** concertos are beautiful.	adjective
10.	He wished to be completely **exculpated**.	adjective

Identify the **part of sentence** in **bold** in each sentence below:

11.	"Rest room" is a **euphemism**.	subject complement
12.	Who was the anonymous **benefactor** to little Pip?	subject complement
13.	A Napoleon complex is a **form** of megalomania.	subject complement
14.	The oil magnates in Saudi Arabia control **billions**.	direct object
15.	Her vivacious personality cheered **us** all.	direct object
16.	The heliotropic vines clogged the **window**.	direct object
17.	There is no **lack** of amour-propre in her!	subject complement
18.	The spry octogenarian won the **race**.	direct object
19.	This **wine** is preferred by the cognoscenti.	subject
20.	He consumed a painful **surfeit** of food and drink.	direct object

For each sentence, identify the type of *phrase* in *italics* and give its part of speech:

1.	He will quickly **delineate** all *of the options*.	prepositional, adverb
2.	*To complicate matters,* the planet moves in a **retrograde** motion.	infinitive, adverb
3.	Some people feel a black **melancholy** *on rainy days*.	prepositional, adverb
4.	*Intracranial meditating* will not exorcise her demons.	gerund, noun
5.	You need **cardiovascular** exercise *to lose weight properly*.	infinitive, adverb
6.	The flash was an **epiphany**, *a sudden appearing of insight*.	appositive, adjective
7.	The blue planet, *a gas giant*, reached **perihelion**.	appositive, adjective
8.	Americans possess an **inherent** right *to free speech*.	prepositional, adjective
9.	Is the national government a **plutocracy**, *sagging under elitism*?	participial, adjective
10.	Money, *the **sine qua non** for acceptance*, was scarce.	appositive, adjective

For each sentence, identify the **sentence structure**. Disregard bold type.

11.	I said that the right/wrong **dichotomy** seemed simplistic.	complex
12.	The fascist dictator was a **pathological** liar; he was evil.	compound
13.	When we looked, we found a **cryptic** inscription in the stone.	complex
14.	He drew an **isosceles** trapezoid on the board, and they understood.	compound
15.	The team's careful search did not locate the **pathogen**.	simple
16.	As we listened, his **vociferous** protests could be heard for blocks.	complex
17.	Please take steps **to rectify** the situation and to make it right.	simple
18.	His **sanctimonious** lectures were hypocritical, but no one noticed.	compound
19.	The **tortuous** mountain highway wound steeply up as we drove.	complex
20.	The insect's **metamorphosis** was miraculous; it was wonderful.	compound

For each of the following sentences, circle the letter of each answer that is true. The answer can be any combination, including all or none. This exercise will teach you the real process of punctuation as a function of grammar.

1. With a rising sense of apprehension my colleague thought Now its time.
   a. a comma after the prepositional phrases
   b. an apostrophe in the contraction
   c. a comma before the direct quotation
   d. quotation marks around the direct quotation
   e. a period inside the closing quotation marks

2. When the poet wrote Silver Mune he recalled Jupiter's ancient epic.
   a. a comma after the independent clause
   b. an apostrophe in the possessive noun
   c. a comma after the dependent clause
   d. italics on the poem title
   e. quotation marks around the poem title

3. A one third minority chose batteries cables and connectors.
   a. a hyphen in the compound adjective
   b. a colon at the beginning of the list
   c. a comma after the plural common noun
   d. a comma before the coordinating conjunction
   e. a comma after the dependent clause

4. Pausing suddenly the venerable grizzled sailor realized its identity.
   a. a comma after the prepositional phrase
   b. a comma between the adjectives preceding the noun
   c. a comma after the participial phrase
   d. a comma after the gerund phrase
   e. an apostrophe in the contraction

5. Pensar is the Spanish verb for think it is a common verb.
   a. quotation marks around the Spanish verb
   b. italics on the Spanish verb
   c. a comma after the independent clause
   d. a comma after the dependent clause
   e. a semicolon after the independent clause

For each of the following sentences, circle the letter of each answer that is true. The answer can be any combination, including all or none. This exercise will teach you the real process of punctuation as a function of grammar.

1. With a rising sense of apprehension, my colleague thought, "Now it's time."
   a. a comma after the prepositional phrases
   b. an apostrophe in the contraction
   c. a comma before the direct quotation
   d. quotation marks around quotation
   e. period inside closing quotation marks

   We put a comma after multiple introductory prepositional phrases.

2. When the poet wrote "Silver Mune," he recalled Jupiter's ancient epic.
   a. a comma after the independent clause
   b. an apostrophe in the possessive noun
   c. a comma after the dependent clause
   d. italics on the poem title
   e. quotation marks around the poem title

   The title of a poem or chapter is in quotation marks; the title of an entire book is in italics.

3. A one-third minority chose batteries, cables, and connectors.
   a. a hyphen in the compound adjective
   b. a colon at the beginning of the list
   c. a comma after the plural common noun
   d. a comma before the coordinating conjunction
   e. a comma after the dependent clause

   We will insist on using comma before the last item in a list, rather than omitting the final comma, as some manuals advise.

4. Pausing suddenly, the venerable, grizzled sailor realized its identity.
   a. a comma after the prepositional phrase
   b. comma between adjectives preceding noun
   c. a comma after the participial phrase
   d. a comma after the gerund phrase
   e. an apostrophe in the contraction

   We separate a list of adjectives preceding a noun, except for the definite or indefinite article. In other words, we would NOT write, "It was the, perspicacious man who called."

5. *Pensar* is the Spanish verb for think; it is a common verb.
   a. quotation marks around the Spanish verb
   b. italics on the Spanish verb
   c. a comma after the independent clause
   d. a comma after the dependent clause
   e. semicolon after independent clause

   We put all foreign language words in italics. This is a compound sentence with an I;I structure.

Use the grammar clues to solve this Mystery Sentence:

A sentence from a fairy tale begins with a proper noun of direct address, used twice, followed by an imperative independent clause containing an understood subject, a present tense transitive verb, an adverb, a second person singular possessive pronoun, and a singular common noun as a direct object. All words are one-syllable words except for the noun of direct address, which contains three syllables.

Rapunzel, Rapunzel, let down your hair.

Identify the **part of speech** in bold in each sentence below:

1.	His **chronic** illness dragged on for years.	adjective
2.	His colorful **hyperbole** livened his conversation.	noun
3.	Dr. King's **sonorous** voice echoed over the crowd.	adjective
4.	Her **germane** comments really hit the mark.	adjective
5.	His **convivial** friends loved to celebrate.	adjective
6.	His **cognomen** is "Huckleberry."	noun
7.	The **anarchist** passed out leaflets to passersby.	noun
8.	Your **animadversions** on his behavior are superfluous.	noun
9.	The deliberate snub was a low, **pusillanimous** act.	adjective
10.	The mayor ducked a question with a clever **subterfuge**.	noun

Identify the *part of sentence* in *italics* in each sentence below.

11.	Her **saturnine** personality won *her* few friends.	indirect object
12.	*They* were forcefully **expatriated** from the fatherland.	subject
13.	Flagpole sitting is a highly **sedentary** *occupation*.	subject complement
14.	He was a popular *fellow* of appealing **bonhomie**.	subject complement
15.	The company will make a **bona fide** *offer*.	direct object
16.	The wealthy **bon vivant** lived the good *life*.	direct object
17.	The **mutable** *laws* of high fashion can't be predicted.	subject
18.	It is *unnecessary* to **impute** evil motives to opponents.	subject complement
19.	It can be *dangerous* to disrupt the **status quo**.	subject complement
20.	The incident offers an instructive *paradigm* for future guidance.	direct object

For each sentence, identify the type of *phrase* in *italics*:

1. The debate created a **schism** *in the Democratic party*. prepositional, adverb

2. His **bootless** effort *to win acceptance* was pathetic. infinitive, adjective

3. *Seized with enthusiasm*, the media created the champ's **apotheosis**. participial, adjective

4. The rumblings were the **precursor** of what was *soon to come*. infinitive, adjective

5. Dyslexics sometimes **transpose** letters *in a word*. prepositional, adjective

6. The Prime Minister, *a veteran*, endured her opponent's **invective**. appositive, adjective

7. The origin of atoms, *a cosmological question*, is unknown. appositive, adjective

8. His **effusion** *of officious greetings* made us wince. prepositional, adjective

9. It was bittersweet *to present a posthumous award*. infinitive, adverb

10. He loved the **euphony** *of the wind in the trees*. prepositional, adjective

For each sentence, identify the **sentence structure**. Disregard bold type.

11. The **refractory** child broke and rebroke the rules. simple

12. We need fresh ideas; we do not need hollow **platitudes**. compound

13. He began to feel **acrophobia**, but he didn't have xenophobia. compound

14. When they first arrive, some visitors feel **agoraphobia**. complex

15. Notice the fable's eerie **verisimilitude** if you can. complex

16. We even loved his many **idiosyncrasies**. simple

17. The government chose to regard the act as **casus belli**. simple

18. The nation survived a peaceful **interregnum**, but it didn't last. compound

19. As you will see, it was an unintentional **infraction** of the rules. complex

20. He will receive a **condign** punishment for his offense. simple

For each of the following sentences, circle the letter of each answer that is true. The answer can be any combination, including all or none. This exercise will teach you the real process of punctuation as a function of grammar.

1. Hail Marching Legions is the song to sing if its a new invasion.
   a. italics on the song title
   b. quotation marks around the song title
   c. a comma before the dependent clause
   d. a comma before the independent clause
   e. an apostrophe in the contraction

2. Yes its mandatory to include three objects in a two dimensional plane.
   a. a comma after the interjection
   b. an apostrophe in the possessive pronoun
   c. an apostrophe in the contraction
   d. a comma after the independent clause
   e. a hyphen in the compound adjective

3. In the Great Dismal Swamp the outbreak of malaria is up by one third.
   a. a comma after the introductory prepositional phrase
   b. a hyphen in the fraction
   c. a comma after the dependent clause
   d. commas around the appositive
   e. commas around the parenthetical remark

4. On September 11 2009 Smithers our ablest engineer designed the new bridge.
   a. a comma after the day
   b. a comma after the year appositive
   c. a comma after the participial phrase
   d. commas around the appositive
   e. a comma after the dependent clause

5. Caught in the blue tube Tashtego reached for the harpoon.
   a. a comma after the dependent clause
   b. a comma after the introductory prepositional phrases
   c. a comma after the participial phrase
   d. commas around the appositive
   e. a semicolon between the clauses

For each of the following sentences, circle the letter of each answer that is true. The answer can be any combination, including all or none. This exercise will teach you the real process of punctuation as a function of grammar.

1. "Hail Marching Legions" is the song to sing if it's a new invasion.
   a. italics on the song title
   b. quotation marks around the song title
   c. a comma before the dependent clause
   d. a comma before the independent clause
   e. an apostrophe in the contraction

   It's is the contraction of it and is, and therefore needs an apostrophe.

2. Yes, it's mandatory to include three objects in a two-dimensional plane.
   a. a comma after the interjection
   b. an apostrophe in the possessive pronoun
   c. an apostrophe in the contraction
   d. a comma after the independent clause
   e. hyphen in the compound adjective

   We do put a comma after an introductory interjection.

3. In the Great Dismal Swamp, the outbreak of malaria is up by one third.
   a. a comma after the introductory prepositional phrase
   b. a hyphen in the fraction
   c. a comma after the dependent clause
   d. commas around the appositive
   e. commas around the parenthetical remark

   Even though this is only a single introductory prepositional phrase, we will put a comma because it is a longer phrase. If the fraction preceded a noun, we would use a hyphen, but in this case, one is just an adjective that modifies its noun third, so no hyphen is needed.

4. On September 11, 2009, Smithers, our ablest engineer, designed the new bridge.
   a. a comma after the day
   b. a comma after the year appositive
   c. a comma after the participial phrase
   d. commas around the appositive
   e. a comma after the dependent clause

   We might first read this as though Smithers were a noun of direct address, but since no answer mentions that, it is a best guess to think that our ablest engineer is an appositive defining Smithers.

5. Caught in the blue tube, Tashtego reached for the harpoon.
   a. a comma after the dependent clause
   b. a comma after the introductory prepositional phrases
   c. a comma after the participial phrase
   d. commas around the appositive
   e. a semicolon between the clauses

   We use commas after introductory participial phrases.

Use the grammar clues to solve this Mystery Sentence:

A famous sentence by Franklin Roosevelt begins with a definite article and an adjective both modifying a singular common noun which is the subject of the clause. This subject is then modified by an interrupting adjective clause containing a first person plural subject pronoun, a present tense action verb, and an infinitive used as an adverb. The main clause then concludes with a present tense linking verb a singular common noun, and a reflexive pronoun.

The only thing we have to fear is fear itself.

Identify the **part of speech** in **bold** in each sentence below:

1.	They had a private **colloquy** in the corner.	noun
2.	**Is** the fetus mature enough to be **viable**?	adjective
3.	Here is a brief **synopsis** of the course.	noun
4.	The argonauts longed to stand on **terra firma** at last.	noun
5.	We cannot **sanction** the use of our name.	verb
6.	The editor was an unapologetic **Russophobe**.	noun
7.	The doctor presented a **prognosis** of the disease.	noun
8.	We purchased a large **polychrome** sculpture.	adjective
9.	Her deeds of **philanthropy** were legendary.	noun
10.	Everyone admired the **perspicacity** of her mind.	noun

Identify the *part of sentence* in *italics* in each sentence below:

11.	The text showed the *mobocracy* of the revolution.	direct object
12.	The Soviet **gerontocracy** is losing *control*.	direct object
13.	His **magniloquent** oratory was *impressive*.	subject complement
14.	The police tried *to arrest a **kleptomaniac***.	direct object
15.	Her *joie de vivre* was inspiring.	subject
16.	The *school* must act **in loco parentis**.	noun
17.	The thinker was *reluctant* to deal with **mundane** matters.	subject complement
18.	He gave a refreshing, **unequivocal** *answer*.	direct object
19.	The icy *nihilism* of his mind could be unnerving.	subject
20.	He paid *one* of them an **invidious** compliment.	indirect object

For each sentence, identify the type of *phrase* in *italics*:

1. *To increase accuracy*, science uses a process of **induction**.   infinitive, adverb

2. *Governed by fear*, the Iranian **hagiocracy** banned swimsuits.   participial, adjective

3. The pedant confined himself *to a scholarly Latin* **diction**.   prepositional, adverb

4. Johnson, *the* **disconsolate** *widower*, missed his wife.   appositive, adjective

5. *His* **disingenuous** *offering* of assistance fooled the ingenue.   gerund, noun

6. The **fractious** mob clamored *to avenge the outrage*.   infinitive, adverb

7. The mendicant, *a plaza regular*, wore a **nondescript** garment.   appositive, adjective

8. The **prolific** writer wrote seven books *in two years*.   prepositional, adverb

9. We read the novel, *a* **chronicle** *of the brave knight-errant*.   appositive, adjective

10. *Crushed into stone*, coal is the remains of a **primeval** forest.   participial, adjective

For each sentence, identify the **sentence structure**. Disregard bold type.

11. The speech was a **panegyric** on her talent; it was effective.   compound

12. Your task is to read Dante's **magnum opus**, the *Divina Comedia*.   simple

13. He loved grandfather's **antediluvian** ideas, and he took his advice.   compound

14. We need to process a customer's request **expeditiously**.   simple

15. The **decadent** century saw little greatness in art as we have seen.   complex

16. His arrogant, **supercilious** manner offended everyone.   simple

17. It is true; her **inexorable** fate followed her everywhere.   compound

18. When dawn broke, they greeted an **emissary** from the Queen.   complex

19. The **improvident** spendthrift went broke, but he recovered.   compound

20. As I said, the **moribund** corporation fired half its work force.   complex

For each of the following sentences, circle the letter of each answer that is true. The answer can be any combination, including all or none. This exercise will teach you the real process of punctuation as a function of grammar.

1. In May the ship reached its darkest moment when a tsunami struck.
   a. a comma after the prepositional phrase
   b. a comma after the month
   c. an apostrophe in the possessive pronoun
   d. an apostrophe in the contraction
   e. a comma between the clauses

2. As the heat wave abated Queequeg leered at the shipmate.
   a. a comma after the participial phrase
   b. a comma after the dependent clause
   c. a comma after the independent clause
   d. a semicolon between the clauses
   e. a comma after the prepositional phrase

3. The double braced hull is tight caulked and dry.
   a. a hyphen in the compound adjective
   b. a colon before the list
   c. a comma after the adjective **tight**
   d. a list comma after the adjective **caulked**
   e. a comma between the clauses

4. Swimming among the whales was the expatriots deepest desire.
   a. a comma after the introductory participial phrase
   b. a comma after the dependent clause
   c. an apostrophe in the possessive noun
   d. commas around the appositive phrase
   e. commas around the parenthetical remark

5. Yeah the expedition found twenty five whales beyond the outer reef.
   a. a comma after the introductory adverb
   b. a comma after the interjection
   c. a comma after the dependent clause
   d. a hyphen in the compound adjective
   e. a comma before the prepositional phrase

For each of the following sentences, circle the letter of each answer that is true. The answer can be any combination, including all or none. This exercise will teach you the real process of punctuation as a function of grammar.

1. In May the ship reached its darkest moment when a tsunami struck.
   a. a comma after the prepositional phrase
   b. a comma after the month
   c. an apostrophe in the possessive pronoun
   d. an apostrophe in the contraction
   e. a comma between the clauses

   No punctuation. When a complex sentence begins with the independent clause, that is when we do not put a comma. The rules are D,I and ID.

2. As the heat wave abated, Queequeg leered at the shipmate.
   a. a comma after the participial phrase
   b. a comma after the dependent clause
   c. a comma after the independent clause
   d. a semicolon between the clauses
   e. a comma after the prepositional phrase

   This is a D,I complex sentence.

3. The double-braced hull is tight, caulked, and dry.
   a. a hyphen in the compound adjective
   b. a colon before the list
   c. a comma after the adjective **tight**
   d. a list comma after the adjective **caulked**
   e. a comma between the clauses

   Here is another list.

4. Swimming among the whales was the expatriots deepest desire.
   a. a comma after the introductory participial phrase
   b. a comma after the dependent clause
   c. an apostrophe in the possessive noun
   d. commas around the appositive phrase
   e. commas around the parenthetical remark

   The gerund phrase Swimming among the whales *is a noun and the subject of the sentence; therefore we should not put a comma after it—that would split the subject off from its verb!*

5. Yeah, the expedition found twenty-five whales beyond the outer reef.
   a. a comma after the introductory adverb
   b. a comma after the interjection
   c. a comma after the dependent clause
   d. a hyphen in the compound adjective
   e. a comma before the prepositional phrase

   We put a comma after an introductory interjection; interjections, after all, have no grammatical function, and are logically separate from the other words. The comma shows this separateness.

The meteor struck, and Leonidas smiled stoically.

1. The word **meteor** is
   a. a noun
   b. a pronoun
   c. an adjective
   d. an interjection

2. The word **Leonidas**
   a. a noun
   b. a plural noun
   c. a common, plural noun
   d. a proper, singular noun

3. The word **stoically** is
   a. an adjective
   b. an adverb
   c. a preposition
   d. a verb

4. The verbs are in
   a. present tense
   b. past tense
   c. a preposition
   d. a verb

5. The sentence is
   a. simple
   b. compound
   c. complex
   d. compound-complex

6. The sentence contains
   a. a direct object
   b. a subject complement
   c. an indirect object
   d. none of the above

7. The sentence contains
   a. one clause
   b. two independent clauses
   c. one dependent clause
   d. no dependent clause

8. The sentence purpose is
   a. declarative
   b. interrogative
   c. imperative
   d. exclamatory

9. **The meteor struck** is
   a. the subject
   b. a gerund phrase
   c. a dependent clause
   d. an independent clause

10. The word **and** is
    a. a subordinating conjunction
    b. a coordinating conjunction
    c. a correlative conjunction
    d. a conjunctive adverb

Attacking and withdrawing are unpleasant alternatives.

11. The word **Attacking** is
   a. a noun
   b. a verb
   c. an adverb
   d. an adjective

12. The word **and** is
   a. a noun
   b. an interjection
   c. a preposition
   d. a conjunction

13. The word **unpleasant** is
   a. a noun
   b. an adjective
   c. an adverb
   d. a common noun

14. The word **alternatives** is
   a. a noun
   b. a common noun
   c. a singular common noun
   d. a plural common noun

15. The word **are** is
   a. a verb
   b. a present tense verb
   c. a present tense linking verb
   d. an action verb

16. The sentence contains
   a. one dependent clause
   b. two dependent clauses
   c. three dependent clauses
   d. none of the above

17. The sentence contains
   a. one gerund
   b. no gerund
   c. one infinitive
   d. two gerunds

18. The sentence structure is
   a. simple
   b. compound
   c. complex
   d. compound-complex

19. The sentence contains a
   a. compound subject
   b. compound predicate
   c. compound direct object
   d. compound subject complement

20. The word **alternatives** is
   a. a direct object
   b. an indirect object
   c. a subject complement
   d. none of the above

Suddenly, the massive hatch slammed down.

21. The word **Suddenly** is an
    a. adjective
    b. adverb
    c. interjection
    d. conjunction

22. The word **hatch** is
    a. a noun
    b. a pronoun
    c. a verb
    d. an adverb

23. The word **down** is
    a. a preposition
    b. an adverb
    c. an adjective
    d. a verb

24. The word **massive** is
    a. a verb
    b. an adverb
    c. a noun
    d. an adjective

25. The verb is in the
    a. present tense
    b. future tense
    c. past tense
    d. past perfect tense

26. The verb is
    a. action
    b. linking
    c. action, past tense
    d. action present tense

27. The verb is
    a. transitive
    b. intransitive
    c. linking
    d. none of the above

28. The sentence purpose is
    a. declarative
    b. imperative
    c. exclamatory
    d. interrogative

29. The sentence structure is
    a. simple
    b. compound
    c. complex
    d. compound-complex

30. The sentence contains
    a. no adverb
    b. one adverb
    c. two adverbs
    d. three adverbs

As the doomed mansion burned, she tried desperately to escape.

31. The word **doomed** is
    a. an adjective
    b. an adverb
    c. an interjection
    d. a preposition

32. The word **she** is
    a. a noun
    b. a pronoun
    c. a verb
    d. an adverb

33. The word **As** is
    a. an adjective
    b. an adverb
    c. a preposition
    d. a conjunction

34. The word **desperately** is
    a. an adjective
    b. an adverb
    c. a verb
    d. an interjection

35. The term **to escape**
    a. is a noun
    b. is an adverb
    c. is an adjective
    d. is a pronoun

36. The sentence contains
    a. a coordinating conjunction
    b. a subordinating conjunction
    c. a correlative conjunction
    d. none of the above

37. The word **mansion** is
    a. proper, plural
    b. proper, singular
    c. common, plural
    d. common, singular

38. The sentence purpose is
    a. declarative
    b. imperative
    c. exclamatory
    d. interrogative

39. The sentence contains
    a. one dependent clause
    b. two dependent clauses
    c. one clause
    d. two independent clauses

40. The sentence structure is
    a. simple
    b. compound
    c. complex
    d. compound-complex

Yesterday, Jupiter was full and unusually bright.

41. The word **bright** is
    a. a noun
    b. an adjective
    c. an adverb
    d. an interjection

42. The word **Jupiter** is
    a. a noun
    b. a pronoun
    c. a proper noun
    d. a proper, singular noun

43. The word **Yesterday** is
    a. a noun
    b. an adjective
    c. an adverb
    d. an interjection

44. The word **full** is
    a. an adjective
    b. an adverb
    c. a noun
    d. a preposition

45. The word **unusually** is
    a. an adjective
    b. an adverb
    c. a conjunction
    d. an interjection

46. The word **unusually** modifies
    a. full
    b. Jupiter
    c. was
    d. bright

47. The word **bright** modifies
    a. Jupiter
    b. was
    c. unusually
    d. full

48. The sentence structure is
    a. simple
    b. compound
    c. complex
    d. compound-complex

49. The sentence purpose is
    a. declarative
    b. imperative
    c. interrogative
    d. exclamatory

50. The sentence contains
    a. one clause
    b. one dependent clause
    c. two clauses
    d. two independent clauses

The meteor struck, and Leonidas smiled stoically.

1. The word **meteor** is
   a. a noun
   b. a pronoun
   c. an adjective
   d. an interjection

2. The word **Leonidas** is
   a. a noun
   b. a plural noun
   c. a common, plural noun
   d. a proper, singular noun

3. The word **stoically** is
   a. an adjective
   b. an adverb
   c. a preposition
   d. a verb

4. The verbs are in
   a. present tense
   b. past tense
   c. a preposition
   d. a verb

5. The sentence is
   a. simple
   b. compound
   c. complex
   d. compound-complex

6. The sentence contains
   a. a direct object
   b. a subject complement
   c. an indirect object
   d. none of the above

7. The sentence contains
   a. one clause
   b. two independent clauses
   c. one dependent clause
   d. no dependent clause

8. The sentence purpose is
   a. declarative
   b. interrogative
   c. imperative
   d. exclamatory

9. **The meteor struck** is
   a. the subject
   b. a gerund phrase
   c. a dependent clause
   d. an independent clause

10. The word **and** is
    a. a subordinating conjunction
    b. a coordinating conjunction
    c. a correlative conjunction
    d. a conjunctive adverb

Attacking and withdrawing are unpleasant alternatives.

11.   The word **Attacking** is
        a. a noun
        b. a verb
        c. an adverb
        d. an adjective

12.   The word **and** is
        a. a noun
        b. an interjection
        c. a preposition
        d. a conjunction

13.   The word **unpleasant** is
        a. a noun
        b. an adjective
        c. an adverb
        d. a common noun

14.   The word **alternatives** is
        a. a noun
        b. a common noun
        c. a singular common noun
        d. a plural common noun

15.   The word **are** is
        a. a verb
        b. a present tense verb
        c. a present tense linking verb
        d. an action verb

16. The sentence contains
        a. one dependent clause
        b. two dependent clauses
        c. three dependent clauses
        d. none of the above

17. The sentence contains
        a. one gerund
        b. no gerund
        c. one infinitive
        d. two gerunds

18. The sentence structure is
        a. simple
        b. compound
        c. complex
        d. compound-complex

19. The sentence contains a
        a. compound subject
        b. compound predicate
        c. compound direct object
        d. compound subject complement

20. The word **alternatives** is
        a. a direct object
        b. an indirect object
        c. a subject complement
        d. none of the above

Suddenly, the massive hatch slammed down.

21. The word **Suddenly** is an
    a. adjective
    b. adverb
    c. interjection
    d. conjunction

22. The word **hatch** is
    a. a noun
    b. a pronoun
    c. a verb
    d. an adverb

23. The word **down** is
    a. a preposition
    b. an adverb
    c. an adjective
    d. a verb

24. The word **massive** is
    a. a verb
    b. an adverb
    c. a noun
    d. an adjective

25. The verb is in the
    a. present tense
    b. future tense
    c. past tense
    d. past perfect tense

26. The verb is
    a. action
    b. linking
    c. action, past tense
    d. action present tense

27. The verb is
    a. transitive
    b. intransitive
    c. linking
    d. none of the above

28. The sentence purpose is
    a. declarative
    b. imperative
    c. exclamatory
    d. interrogative

29. The sentence structure is
    a. simple
    b. compound
    c. complex
    d. compound-complex

30. The sentence contains
    a. no adverb
    b. one adverb
    c. two adverbs
    d. three adverbs

As the doomed mansion burned, she tried desperately to escape.

31. The word **doomed** is
    a. an adjective
    b. an adverb
    c. an interjection
    d. a preposition

32. The word **she** is
    a. a noun
    b. a pronoun
    c. a verb
    d. an adverb

33. The word **As** is
    a. an adjective
    b. an adverb
    c. a preposition
    d. a conjunction

34. The word **desperately** is
    a. an adjective
    b. an adverb
    c. a verb
    d. an interjection

35. The term **to escape**
    a. is a noun
    b. is an adverb
    c. is an adjective
    d. is a pronoun

36. The sentence contains
    a. a coordinating conjunction
    b. a subordinating conjunction
    c. a correlative conjunction
    d. none of the above

37. The word **mansion** is
    a. proper, plural
    b. proper, singular
    c. common, plural
    d. common, singular

38. The sentence purpose is
    a. declarative
    b. imperative
    c. exclamatory
    d. interrogative

39. The sentence contains
    a. one dependent clause
    b. two dependent clauses
    c. one clause
    d. two independent clauses

40. The sentence structure is
    a. simple
    b. compound
    c. complex
    d. compound-complex

Yesterday, Jupiter was full and unusually bright.

41. The word **bright** is
    a. a noun
    b. an adjective
    c. an adverb
    d. an interjection

42. The word **Jupiter** is
    a. a noun
    b. a pronoun
    c. a proper noun
    d. a proper, singular noun

43. The word **Yesterday** is
    a. a noun
    b. an adjective
    c. an adverb
    d. an interjection

44. The word **full** is
    a. an adjective
    b. an adverb
    c. a noun
    d. a preposition

45. The word **unusually** is
    a. an adjective
    b. an adverb
    c. a conjunction
    d. an interjection

46. The word **unusually** modifies
    a. full
    b. Jupiter
    c. was
    d. bright

47. The word **bright** modifies
    a. Jupiter
    b. was
    c. unusually
    d. full

48. The sentence structure is
    a. simple
    b. compound
    c. complex
    d. compound-complex

49. The sentence purpose is
    a. declarative
    b. imperative
    c. interrogative
    d. exclamatory

50. The sentence contains
    a. one clause
    b. one dependent clause
    c. two clauses
    d. two independent clauses